Jesus'
Final
Warning

Jesus' Final Warning

HEARING THE SAVIOR'S VOICE IN THE MIDST OF CHAOS

David Jeremiah

WORD PUBLISHING

NASHVILLE

A Thomas Nelson Company

Unless otherwise noted, Scripture quotations are from THE NEW KING JAMES VER-SION. Copyright © 1979, 1980, 1982, Thomas Nelson, Inc.

Scripture quotations noted KJV are from the KING JAMES VERSION of the Bible.

Scripture quotations noted MSG are from *The Message: The New Testament in Contemporary English*. Copyright © 1993 by Eugene H. Peterson. Used by permission of NavPress Publishing Group.

Scripture quotations noted NASB are from the NEW AMERICAN STANDARD BIBLE, Copyright © The Lockman Foundation 1960, 1962, 1963, 1968, 1971, 1972, 1973, 1975, 1977. Used by permission.

Scripture quotations noted NIV are from the HOLY BIBLE: NEW INTERNATIONAL VERSION. Copyright © 1973, 1978, 1984 by International Bible Society. Used by permission of Zondervan Publishing House. All rights reserved.

Scripture quotations noted PHILLIPS are from J. B. Phillips: *The New Testament in Modern English*, Revised Edition. Copyright © J. B. Phillips 1958, 1960, 1972. Used by permission of Macmillan Publishing Co., Inc.

Scripture quotations noted TLB are from *The Living Bible*, copyright © 1971. Used by permission of Tyndale House Publishers, Inc., Wheaton, Illinois 60189. All rights reserved.

Library of Congress Cataloging-in-Publication Data

Jeremiah, David.
    Jesus' final warning: hearing the Savior's voice in the midst of
chaos / David Jeremiah.
      p. cm.
    Includes bibliographical references.
    ISBN 0-8499-1518-X
    1. Jesus Christ—Prophecies.   I. Title.
BT370.J47   1999
232.9'54—dc21   99-24305
                                                                   CIP

Dedication

⸺◦◦◦⸺

To my father, Dr. James T. Jeremiah,
who for over sixty years has faithfully
proclaimed the Word of God.

Contents

Acknowledgments

First of all, at the center of my life is my wonderful Savior who gives me life energy and motivation, whose written Word fills my mind and heart with thoughts that I cannot keep to myself.

My wife, Donna, knows my passion to communicate the Word of God and during the long hours in which a book is being created, she not only understands, she cheers me on. This has been her consistent practice for the thirty-six years of our marriage. How blessed I am!

Our team at Shadow Mountain Community Church and at the Turning Point Ministries have also encouraged me. Glenda Parker, my administrative assistant at the church has served me in this capacity for eighteen years and continues to handle the myriads of details that could clutter up my mind and keep me from the uninterrupted periods of study that are the making of messages and books.

Helen Barnhart serves in a similar capacity at Turning Point. She keeps things organized in my office there and her giftedness with-the computer saves me hours of time both in preparation of the manuscript and coordination of its publication.

Once again, Steve Halliday and Larry Libby of Crown Media have added their elegant touch to the editing of the manuscript.

Sealy Yates, my personal friend and literary agent, wonderfully represents me to our publishers and faithfully represents them to me as well.

Finally I want to express my appreciation to the people at Word Publishing for their continued confidence and trust. To Ernie Owen, Joey Paul, Lee Gessner, and the rest of the team at Word . . . thank you for praying for me these last months and for working so hard to make *Jesus' Final Warning* a project that will bring honor and glory to our Lord!

David Jeremiah
April, 1999

One

HEARING THE MASTER'S VOICE IN
THE MIDST OF MILLENNIAL MADNESS

At regular intervals throughout world history, fear of what might happen in the future has prompted many individuals to latch onto a particular date and plan some radical action to take on or before that date.

Back in 1843, for example, a New Englander named William Miller came to ardently believe in the imminent return of Jesus Christ. Unfortunately, he began to speculate about the date of that return using some dubious mathematical calculations. He collected mounds of data, analyzed it, and was certain he had made no mistakes. He therefore confidently announced to his followers that on March 21, 1843, Jesus Christ would return to the earth.

Historical records tell us that a comet streaking across the night sky helped to confirm Miller in his delusions. At midnight on the appointed day, his devoted followers donned their ascension robes, trekked into the mountains, and climbed towering trees to get as high as possible so they would have "less distance to travel through the air" when the Lord returned to take them home.

But the day came and went. The Lord did not return. And the trees became awfully uncomfortable.

And so a dejected band of Millerites trudged home to a late breakfast on March 22, accompanied by the jeers and catcalls of their neighbors and "friends." It was a sad and bitter day for these deeply disappointed men and women.

But William Miller was not a man to give up easily. He immediately went back to the Scriptures and found a "mistake" in his calculations. Why, he had miscounted by one year! So it was that, 365 days later, the Millerites once again robed themselves, climbed trees, and awaited the Lord's return.

And once again, they were disappointed.

By this point, the angry Millerites had had enough. You can clean twigs out of your hair and bear vicious mocking for only so long. William Miller's followers quickly dwindled to almost nothing. Most of his disciples turned their hearts away from their sincere but deluded leader—and infinitely more tragic, turned their hearts away from God.

To his credit, Miller himself soon repented of his date-setting and publicly admitted he had made a terrible error not merely in his calculations, but in his foolish attempts to name the date of Christ's return. But by then, of course, he had demolished his credibility along with the faith of many of his erstwhile followers.

The Story Continues

Our own generation has seen many "important" dates come and go. The fortieth anniversary of Israel's founding as a modern nation occurred in 1988, and that event seemed to spur a number of predictions about the imminent end of the world. Certain individuals insisted that a biblical "generation" consisted of forty years, then pointed to our Lord's prediction in Matthew 24 that He would return before the demise of the generation that saw the rebirth of Israel (Matthew 24:32–34).

Edgar Whisenant picked up on this bit of speculative reasoning and published a little book titled *88 Reasons Why the Rapture Will Be in 1988.* He used a peculiar mix of facts about ancient Israel's major feasts and data about ancient and modern calendars to conclude that Christ would return that September. His book created a furor of interest and sold 4.5 *million* copies in this country, plus an unknown number in several foreign language editions. I somehow got on this man's mailing list and received five copies of his book.

But that book is no longer on the shelves of any library. Why not? Because 1988 came and went, and the Lord Jesus did not return.

This obvious and discouraging fact did not deter Whisenant, however. Taking a page from Miller's book, Whisenant announced that he had miscalculated by one year and quickly wrote another book, *Final Shout,* in which he predicted Jesus would return in 1989.

Of course, he was wrong again. (But at least his followers didn't have to yank twigs out of their hair.)

In 1992, building contractor turned radio evangelist Harold Camping published his own prediction about when the Lord would return. In a book titled *1994?,* he tried to build a case explaining why Jesus would come for His own sometime in September of that year, probably on the sixth. When September came and went, Camping said he could have erred, and said the Lord might return as late as October 2. But again God refused to honor these "calculations," and Jesus continued to remain at His Father's side in heaven.

One disappointed Camping follower, Alvin Allen of Claymont, Delaware, told a newspaper reporter, "We are still trying to understand it. None of this was random. We didn't just pick dates out of nowhere. It all came from the Bible." The reporter slyly added, "The Bible as interpreted by Harold Camping."[1]

The Challenge of Millennial Madness

Today we stand on the threshold of a new millennium. Once again the prophecy books are multiplying and the talk shows are busily chatting about the frightening implications of the year 2000. About three years before M-Day, *Publisher's Weekly* wrote, "Trade publishers will release books calculated to appeal to broad popular audiences by tapping into millennial anxieties. This epochal change stimulates the biggest questions: Is the end of the world near? Are we on the edge of Apocalypse? If so, what will that mean for the human race?"[2] And it concluded, "The potent year of 2000 . . . and perhaps a decade or so beyond—may prove a marketing bonanza, in religion and in other categories, with prophets leading publishers to profits."[3]

Yet this time around there really is an important problem for us to tackle. My friend Larry Burkett wrote a 1998 article for *Turning Point* magazine on the dilemma commonly known as "Y2K" (which stands for "Year Two Thousand"). Burkett wrote:

Most mainframe computers—and a significant number of personal computers—use two digits rather than four to indicate the year. For example, to these computers 1998 is simply "98."

When the year 2000 arrives, the year designation will read "00." Many computers will assume that 00 means 1900 and will start generating erroneous data or shut down entirely.

Experts say the possible fallout from the two missing digits could range from minor inconveniences to an economic recession.

According to one author, who is involved with the House Banking Committee, "the millennium bug 'could mean errors in checking account transactions, interest calculations, or payment schedules. It could mean problems with the ATM systems or credit and debit cards. It could affect bank record keeping, investments, currency transfers,'" etc.

Because most of our economy is computer-dependent, widespread computer malfunctions could cripple normal economic activity. A small-scale example of what could happen occurred just a few months ago when two U.S. railroads, Union Pacific and Southern Pacific, merged. Unfortunately, their computer systems couldn't communicate.

Bumper crops of grain ended up being stranded in the Midwest, California ports were clogged with items that couldn't go anywhere, and production of everything from steel to petrochemicals had to come to a halt—all because of a computer glitch at one company.[4]

Do you realize how dependent our culture has become on computers? If you multiply the problems caused by the railroad computer glitch by millions of businesses worldwide, you begin to understand why "millennial madness" has again become such a concern. The "millennial bug" greatly worries many experts who have been warning us about it for years.

"Well, why don't they just fix it?" somebody says. "We can fix everything. We have all kinds of intellectual ability. Three decades ago we sent a man to the moon. Can't we fix a simple computer glitch?"

The problem is the enormity of the job. Between now and January 1, 2000, billions of lines of computer code must be repaired, one line at a time. Everything has to be tested repeatedly to assure that no glitches remain. One man has said it's like trying to replace every rivet on the Golden Gate Bridge at the same instant during rush hour.

And the biggest problems may be with governmental computers around the globe. A January 1999 article in *Time* magazine titled, "The End of the World As We Know It?" declared,

No one really knows how bad things will get until the witching hour arrives. The Pentagon insists that 95% of its "mission critical" computers will be fixed by June and all of them before Dec. 31. But nuclear weapons systems in all nations—including Russia, where the state of Y2K preparations is anybody's guess—are computer dependent. In November the British American Security Information Council, a nuclear disarmament group, warned that a Y2K glitch could lead to erroneous early—warning reports or even trigger the accidental launch of a nuclear missile. Nuclear power plants could be vulnerable to the same difficulties. Last year, when the Nuclear Regulatory Commission looked at the Seabrook plant in New Hampshire, it found that Y2K problems, unless fixed, would affect the computers that monitored such crucial functions as reactor-coolant levels and fuel-handling systems.[5]

The new millennial madness feeds off such valid concerns. A lot of folks believe that when the year 2000 dawns, we could well witness the end of this age. They think the Y2K computer crisis may signal the approaching return of Jesus Christ to earth. Some other Christians, such as reconstructionist theologian Gary North, have taught that the Y2K problem is God's judgment on a prideful human race. He writes (and clearly hopes) that in the chaos he predicts will follow January 1, 2000, believers will begin to "take dominion" over the governmental institutions of the world, bringing in a new age dominated by the church and characterized by worldwide adherence to "God's moral law." "In all of man's history, we have never been able to predict with such accuracy a worldwide disaster of this magnitude," North has warned. "The millennium clock keeps ticking. There is nothing we can do."[6]

Now, I've read my Bible from beginning to end, and I have yet to find the word *computer* in there. I've checked my concordance, and *Y2K* simply doesn't show up in the biblical text.

But I have found some principles about how we should conduct ourselves in this great transitional time in history.

All my life I have believed that the coming of the Lord is drawing near, and I am still convinced He could return at any moment.

If this time in history causes men and women to stop for a moment and think seriously about what the Word of God has to say about the return of Christ, then I for one will thank the Lord for it. It would be just fine with me if He came back in 2000. In fact, as far as I'm concerned, He doesn't have to wait that long. He has promised He could come at any time, and I say, "The sooner the better."

So Many Voices

We hear so many voices. So many arguments. So many speculations. Everyone has a theory, an idea. And I'm not just talking about CBN, radio and TV talk shows, books and magazines, hundreds of websites, and *USA Today*. All of them are pushing some slant on the millennium issue—and of course, their slants vary widely depending on who's pushing them. So how do you sort through all of this? How do you decide what to believe about the future?

I'd like to suggest there is one slant we ought to trust more than other slants, one "take" we ought to prefer above all other "takes," one opinion we ought to value more than all other opinions. Amid the thousands of shrill voices screaming for our attention, there is but one voice we need to hear.

The voice of the Lord Jesus Christ.

"But what does *He* have to say about the future?" you may ask. It may surprise you to discover how much He does have to say about the future. *Your* future.

What Jesus Said About the Future

The future did not trouble Jesus, nor was He preoccupied with what might happen. The Gospels make it clear that Jesus, more than anyone else who ever walked this planet, knew what the future held, both for Himself personally and for the world at large. We can confidently make four claims about Jesus' relationship to the future.

1. *Jesus Often Referred to the Future*

Jesus frequently spoke of future events in His discussions and discourses. In the Olivet Discourse recorded in Matthew 24:25, for example, Jesus laid out a vision of events to come and concluded by saying to His disciples: "See, I have told you beforehand." He wanted them to know ahead of time some facts to help them (and us) face the coming days.

In Mark 13:23 He said something similar: "But take heed; see, I have told you all things beforehand." Jesus was in the habit of preparing us for the future even during His days upon this earth. He made a point of telling those around Him some of the things they could anticipate in the days ahead. So don't let anyone tell you that Jesus didn't bother about the future. The facts speak otherwise. Jesus talked about the future a great deal.

2. *Jesus Rebuked People for Not Knowing About the Future*

Jesus not only spoke many times about the future, He also reprimanded and rebuked the people because they didn't seem to recognize that important prophesied events were taking place all around them. He once scolded members of a crowd, saying that while they could read the clouds and tell when it was going to rain, although they could look at the winds blowing through their fields and decide when hot weather was approaching, somehow they were unable to read the signs of the times. And He reprimanded them, "Hypocrites! You can discern the face of the sky and of the earth, but how is it you do not discern this time?" (Luke 12:56).

It was no small thing to Jesus that the people of His generation remained ignorant of God's prophetic Word. He expected them to be able to open their eyes, look around, and put two and two together . . . but He found they hadn't even learned their numbers.

What does this mean for us? For one thing, if someone comes to you and says, "I'm not really interested in prophecy. I'm not interested in all of this future stuff," you should read Luke 12:56 to him or her.

Then point out how Jesus used the word *hypocrite* to describe a person who attaches more significance to predictions of the weather than to predictions of the Word.

The Bible instructs us to *always* be looking for the day of Christ's return, not with wild-eyed speculations fueled by our own Millerite "calculations," but with sober and Spirit-led discernment. What else would the Bible mean when it says, "And let us consider one another in order to stir up love and good works, not forsaking the assembling of ourselves together, as is the manner of some, but exhorting one another, *and so much the more as you see the Day approaching*" (Hebrews 10:24–25, emphasis added)? How can we "see the Day approaching" if we aren't even looking for it?

We are to investigate what the Bible has to say and ask God to help us determine the day and the hour in which we live. We cannot remain ignorant of "the signs of the times" simply because thoughts of the future may make us uncomfortable.

3. Jesus Related Future Truth to Present Situations

A pastor friend of mine once asked if I was continuing to study prophecy and preach on it. "Yes," I replied.

"Well," he said, "I've quit doing that."

"Why?" I asked.

"You know what, Jeremiah?" he said. "I've come to the conclusion that prophecy just isn't relevant to our day. It doesn't have anything to do with where people are today in their contemporary situations. People have so many needs and so many hurts—it seems a shame to spend time showing them prophecy charts and talking about the future and all of that."

Such "wisdom" may sound good and prudent and practical, but it ignores one enormous fact: *Every time Jesus talked about the future, He connected it to the present.* The prophecies of the New Testament are constantly undergirded with strong encouragements and admonitions about how we are to live today.

In preparing to write this book, I canvassed the New Testament and was reminded again of how the Lord used truth about the future to encourage and instruct His disciples about their present-day lives.

For example, consider John 14:1–3: "Let not your heart be troubled; you believe in God, believe also in Me. In My Father's house are many mansions; if it were not so, I would have told you. I go to prepare a place for you. And if I go and prepare a place for you, I will come again and receive you to Myself; that where I am, there you may be also." Here Jesus connected His ascension and return—both future events at the time He spoke these words—to His disciples' current experience of peace. He believed that by telling His followers what lay in their future, they would be strengthened to live more vibrantly in the present.

Or consider what the Master said in John 16:1: "These things I have spoken to you [about the future], that you should not be made to stumble." In other words, "Men, if you grasp what I am telling you about the future, you won't fall all over yourself. You won't fall into the trap of running around in panic mode when you have no reason to be in panic mode."

In John 16:4 Jesus said this: "These things I have told you, that when the time comes, you may remember that I told you of them." The days are coming when the hand of God will move across this globe in astounding ways. If we know the Word of God, we won't be taken by surprise. We won't find ourselves in a panic or gripped by sudden apprehensions. Jesus said, in effect, "I've told you about these things so that when they happen, you won't be blown off course. You will have a sense of what God is up to."

This element of Jesus' teaching has greatly shaped the direction of this book. If you are looking for a manual to the future that places no demands upon you today, a guidebook for days to come that has no bearing on days right now, you have come to the wrong place. I can't get excited about any book that inspires concern about future events but ignores what God wants us to do today. My study of prophecy convinces me that God intends knowledge of future events to help us "occupy" with a sense of urgency until the Lord returns.

4. Jesus Revealed the Future So That His Disciples Would Rest in Him

Remember the article by Larry Burkett quoted earlier? By the end of the article Burkett didn't give any answers to the problem he had highlighted. But he did say what I think is the crux of the issue: "When you don't know what the answer is, you know *Who* the answer is."[7]

That is so good! When you don't know how everything is going to work out—and with the Y2K problem, no one really does—you have to hold tightly to the Lord God Himself and trust in the Lord Jesus Christ. We're told to "rest" in the Lord. That is the message we find throughout the New Testament.

At the end of the vitally important sixteenth chapter of John, Jesus says to His disciples, "These things I have spoken to you, that in Me you may have peace. In the world you will have tribulation; but be of good cheer, I have overcome the world" (v. 33).

Throughout that chapter Jesus talks about the future and what is about to happen. He warns His disciples about His imminent death, about the persecution to come, about the sorrow and pain and hardship lying just ahead. But after predicting all these frightful events He says, in effect, "Don't get caught up in that. Make sure that in the midst of these tumultuous times you place your trust wholly in Me."

If you have put your faith in Christ and have spent significant time in the Word of God, the tough times can be like a magnet that draws you to the Lord Jesus. Nothing is going to happen in the year 2000 (or even in the *real* new millennium, which is actually the year 2001) that will catch Jesus Christ by surprise. He is able to help His children work through anything, and not a single thing is going to happen in the future that can change that fact.

So rather than spending all your time reading the magazines and trying to figure the nuances of what the future might hold, maybe you should spend at least as much time getting to know Him better. Then when the future becomes the present, you will enjoy a wondrously close relationship with almighty God and you can be walking with the Lord Jesus Christ in strength. No matter what happens.

Why Should We Hear Jesus' Words Above All Others'?

Jesus talked a lot about the future, He rebuked His listeners for not knowing about the future, He related the future to present-day living, and He told His disciples about the future to encourage them to rest in Him in tough times.

Fair enough. But why should we listen to Him? Why should we read our Bibles more than we read the futuristic magazines and scan the new millennium websites?

In the last week I received four books about the future of the church, the world, and business. It would be incredibly easy to spend all of your time reading the truckloads of futuristic books published each week—and if you did, you would quickly grow confused, because no two of them agree about the shape of what's to come. There's no certain help there.

But why should we listen to the Lord Jesus? Why should we trust what *He* says? Why should we hear His words above those of anyone else? Why should we study our Bibles, especially the Gospels where Jesus speaks about what He wants us to know concerning the future?

If you have placed your faith in Jesus Christ for salvation, the most obvious answer is, "Because we're Christians." If our Savior explicitly says He wants us to know certain things about what lies ahead, we would be incredibly foolish to ignore Him. But beyond that, I think there are at least five reasons why we ought to be eager to hear His counsel on the future.

1. Because of Who He Is

Who is Jesus? He is the Son of God and the Son of man. He is the

God-man and the man-God. He is the Messiah, the Son of the living God. He is God walking around in a body. He is God forever enthroned in heaven at the right hand of the Father. Jesus Christ is God in the flesh.

You can find one of the greatest illustrations of who He is and why we should listen to His words in the prologue to the book of Revelation. The writer of that book, John, was on the Isle of Patmos on the Lord's Day. He saw this One to whom we should listen and he said, "When I saw Him, I fell at His feet as dead. But He laid His right hand on me, saying to me, 'Do not be afraid; I am the First and the Last. I am He who lives, and was dead, and behold, I am alive forevermore. Amen. And I have the keys of Hades and of Death. Write the things which you have seen, and the things which are, and the things which will take place after this'" (Revelation 1:17–19).

Who else do you know who has one foot planted in eternity and the other planted in time? Who else do you know who has been to the future and who therefore says to us today, "This is what you should expect will happen in the days ahead"?

There is no one like Jesus Christ!

No one who has ever lived or ever will live has a grasp of the future even remotely as firm and complete as the Lord Jesus Christ. As God, He alone lives in the time about which He speaks. God lives in all of time as if it were the present. He sees the whole parade of history from beginning to end. We see little snatches of it, but God Almighty sees it all—and Jesus Christ as God tells us what to expect.

We should listen to the Lord Jesus Christ because of who He is. He is the One you can trust. He is the God-man. He is the Son of God, the eternal One, the Alpha and the Omega, the Beginning and the End, the First and the Last.

2. Because of What He Said

Throughout the New Testament Jesus prophesied of future events. These are prophecies we can go back and check, not only through the

Word of God, but through secular history. And we can ask: Can we trust Jesus when He speaks?

I think one of the most amazing of Jesus' prophecies concerned the destruction of the temple in Jerusalem. When He made this prediction, His prophecy must have seemed totally off the wall. We read about it in Matthew 24:1–2:

> Then Jesus went out and departed from the temple, and His disciples came to Him to show Him the buildings of the temple. And Jesus said to them, "Do you not see all these things? Assuredly, I say to you, not one stone shall be left here upon another, that shall not be thrown down."

This statement must have sounded absurd to the men and women who heard Jesus utter these unsettling words. At the time of Jesus' ministry, the temple was undoubtedly one of the most awesome structures in the world. Its builders didn't use mortar as we do today, but instead used massive blocks of stone—some measuring 40 feet by 12 feet by 12 feet—so expertly cut that they fit perfectly against one another in a kind of lock and key system.

The temple buildings were made of gleaming white marble and the entire eastern wall of the main temple structure was covered with gold plates so that it could be seen from the east as the sun rose and the plates glinted its light. It was the most spectacular, breathtaking structure imaginable, magnificent by any day's standards . . . and the disciples couldn't grasp the concept that the whole breathtaking complex would soon become a pile of rubble.

As they walked around the buildings, pointing out their magnificence, they couldn't help saying to Jesus, "Isn't this a great temple that Herod built?" And Jesus couldn't help but reply, "Are you really so impressed with all these gleaming buildings? Let Me tell you something. The time is soon coming when everything you see here will become nothing more than a smoking ruin. The huge blocks of stone that now fit together so precisely will be strewn about the ground, broken and ugly and charred."

The disciples couldn't imagine what kind of cataclysm it would take to obliterate the place, but Jesus knew the history of the site long before humans would record what happened. In fact, in A.D. 70, the Roman general Titus built large wooden scaffolds around the walls of the temple buildings—a tactic never before used. He piled the scaffolds high with wood and other flammable items and set them on fire. The heat from the fires grew so intense that the very stones crumbled, and eventually Roman soldiers sifted through the rubble to retrieve any of the gold that had melted into the smoldering ruins. All that remained on the site was flattened rock … just as Jesus had predicted.

What is the statistical probability that Jesus' prophecy would be fulfilled so literally? The number boggles the mind. But when Jesus speaks, odds mean nothing. What He predicts comes true. What He prophesies happens. Exactly as He says it will.

Or consider another, more short-term, prophecy of our Lord. One day Peter was boasting to the Lord about his faithfulness. "Even if all are made to stumble because of You," he bragged, "I will never be made to stumble." And Jesus replied, "Assuredly, I say to you that this night, before the rooster crows, you will deny Me three times" (Matthew 26:33–34).

Peter was just about the most unpredictable person you could imagine. His mood swings and emotional flip-flops were legendary. If the Lord wanted to pick somebody who was predictable, He surely would have chosen someone other than Peter. The big fisherman was the most unpredictable disciple He could have named! But the Lord knew what the future held for Peter, and exactly what Jesus predicted took place:

Now Peter sat outside in the courtyard. And a servant girl came to him, saying, "You also were with Jesus of Galilee." But he denied it before them all, saying, "I do not know what you are saying." And when he had gone out to the gateway, another girl saw him and said to those who were there, "This fellow also was with Jesus of Nazareth." But again he denied with an oath, "I do not know the Man!" And after a while those who stood by came to Him and said to Peter, "Surely you also are one of them, because your speech betrays you." Then he began to curse and swear, saying, "I do not know the Man!" And immediately a rooster crowed. (Matthew 26:69–74)

Jesus was dead-on in His prophecy, and suddenly Peter realized it. Matthew concludes this section of his Gospel by reporting, "And Peter remembered the word of Jesus who had said to him, 'Before the rooster crows, you will deny Me three times.' Then he went out and wept bitterly" (Matthew 26:75).

Once again, Jesus' words were fulfilled exactly as He said they would be.

Or consider one more prediction, given just before His death. Jesus proclaimed that everyone who had followed Him closely would scatter and flee when He was arrested and crucified. He predicted, "All of you will be made to stumble because of Me this night, for it is written: 'I will strike the Shepherd, and the sheep of the flock will be scattered'" (Matthew 26:31).

Just a few short hours later Jesus was arrested and taken away. Matthew reports, "Then all the disciples forsook Him and fled" (26:56). Just as Jesus had prophesied.

My friend, whenever Jesus speaks, He is always on target. He passed the Old Testament requirement that a true prophet be 100 percent accurate (Deuteronomy 18:22). God does not grade on a curve when it comes to prophecy. A prophet who gets 95 percent of his predictions right cannot be considered a good prophet. According to the Word of God, if a prophet does not get his predictions *completely* right, he cannot qualify as a prophet from God. Because Jesus was *the* Prophet (see Deuteronomy 18:15, 18), He was right on target every time He spoke.

Jesus was just as accurate about His own death and resurrection as He was about the temple and Peter and His disciples. Predictions of His crucifixion and burial are found in all of the Gospels, but consider just a few in the book of Matthew. "From that time Jesus began to show to His disciples that He must go to Jerusalem, and suffer many things from the elders and chief priests and scribes, and be killed, and be raised again the third day" (16:21).

Think about that for a moment. Anyone could have prophesied that he was going to be killed in three days; just raise a ruckus and somebody will get mad enough to kill you. But "just anyone" could *not* say, "After three days, I am going to come out of the grave." Yet Jesus consistently said exactly that. He declared, "As Jonah was three days and three nights in the belly of the great fish, so will the Son of Man be three days and three nights in the heart of the earth" (Matthew 12:40). This prediction, like every other prediction Jesus made, came true. We should listen to Jesus when He speaks of the future because everything He says about events to come is absolutely on target.

3. Because of How He Lived

Whom are you more likely to trust, an honest man or a proven liar? A man of integrity or a man of deceit? A man who looks out for others or a man who looks out for himself? A man who seeks to please God or a man who seeks to please himself? A man driven by his relationship to the Father or a man driven by his lust for material gain?

Jesus is the only Man who ever lived on planet Earth who never sinned. Not once. He never lied. Never stole. Never even lusted. In one of His confrontations with the Pharisees, He threw out a challenge that would make modern journalists salivate. "Which of you convicts Me of sin?" He asked them (John 8:46).

Remember presidential candidate Gary Hart of several years ago? He threw out a challenge like that to the press when they questioned him on his alleged romantic dalliances outside of marriage. He dared journalists to prove he had committed this sin-and soon the papers were full of grainy photographs of Hart in compromising situations with a secret girlfriend. How different when we come to Jesus! He challenged His critics, "Which of you convicts Me of sin?"—and they remained silent. They had nothing to say. Why? Because they *couldn't* convict Him of sin.

The apostle Peter put it like this: "Christ . . . committed no sin, nor was guile found in His mouth" (1 Peter 2:21–22). The apostle Paul wrote that God made Christ "who knew no sin to be sin for us, that we might become the righteousness of God in Him" (2 Corinthians 5:21). We ought to pay close attention to what Jesus says because He is the only person in history who never committed an offense against God. Such a person deserves our full attention.

But it wasn't merely that Jesus never committed a sin! He not only kept himself from engaging in evil, He also continually acted in ways that honored and glorified God. He not only continually avoided the negative, He always pursued the positive. Everything He did, He did to honor His Father. As He said, "I always do those things that please Him" (John 8:29). How can you ignore the words of such a person?

Think of the most godly person you know. Can you see his or her face in your mind's eye right now? What is it that attracts you to this man or woman? His or her kindness? Honesty? Integrity? Faithfulness? Wisdom? Gentleness? Strength? Whatever it is, Jesus possessed that godly characteristic to the nth degree. All the qualities and character that your godly friend possesses are on loan from the Son of God, the very Fountain of integrity and truth. We should listen to His words about the future because they came from lips that never spoke a lie and always glorified God.

4. Because of How He Loves Us

The Bible tells us that Jesus is our Shepherd, that He wants to guide us into the future. He is our Captain Who has gone before us.

He loves us! And we know He loves us by what He did for us. In John 10:11 Jesus says, "I am the good shepherd. The good shepherd gives His life for the sheep." Matthew 9:36 tells us that when Jesus "saw the multitudes, He was moved with compassion for them, because they were weary and scattered, like sheep having no shepherd."

Do you feel weary today? Do thoughts of an uncertain future make you feel anxious, worried, nervous? Does your life seem scattered, out of control, and frenetic? If so, you need to listen closely to the words of Jesus, the Good Shepherd. He knows the future. More particularly, He knows *your* future. And even now He is filled with compassion for you as one of His sheep. Isn't it time you listened for His calm, gentle voice?

5. Because of What He Did for Us

Do you know why I believe in the Lord Jesus and what He says? Because He has proved to me that He has my best interests at heart. What could He do that He did not do? He already gave His life for us. Romans 5:8–10 says it this way: "God demonstrates His own love toward us, in that while we were still sinners, Christ died for us. Much more then, having now been justified by His blood, we shall be saved from wrath through Him. For if when we were enemies we were reconciled to God through the death of His Son, much more, having been reconciled, we shall be saved by His life." And Romans 8:32 adds, "He who did not spare His own Son, but delivered Him up for us all, how shall He not with Him also freely give us all things?"

You can trust the One who died for you. He has proved beyond any reasonable doubt His great love for those who are His children. What He said He would do He always did, and the things we already see fulfilled in His Word simply remind us that what He said about the future will take place just as surely.

Hear His Voice

My friend, if you do not know this One about whom we speak, this voice above all voices, the most important thing for you to do is to enter into a personal relationship with Him. It is not enough to go to church. If I thought all we needed to do to get to heaven was to go to church, I would grab people and throw them in the door of the church just as fast as I could, and once I got them in, I would say, "That's another one!"

But the real issue involves something quite different from that. The real issue is not singing hymns or doing volunteer work; it isn't even knowing the Bible. *It is knowing Jesus Christ.* Jesus is the One who said, "I have come that they may have life, and that they may have it more abundantly" (John 10:10).

Jesus gave His life for you, and if you will give Him your trust, not only will He give you today, He will give you the future. You can walk into that future with His hand in yours, brimming with confidence and without fear, knowing that He is your refuge and your strength.

"Do not fear, little flock, for it is your Father's good pleasure to give you the kingdom," He said in Luke 12:32. Y2K or not, His promise still stands. And remember: Jesus' promises have a way of coming true!

Part One

WARNINGS

Two

DO NOT BE DECEIVED

Since I began my research for this book, I've read more than I ever cared to about the world of computers and the Y2K challenge rushing toward us as we approach the new millennium. Concern over this challenge runs rampant in some circles as men and women worry about what will happen the moment the calendar turns over to the year 2000.

This past week, someone sent me the ultimate solution:

It has been determined that there will no longer be a need for computers or any network of any kind because the goal is to remove all computers from the desktops by January 1999. Instead, everyone will be provided with an Etch-A-Sketch.

There are many sound reasons for doing this: (1) No Y2K problems; (2) No technical glitches keeping work from being done; (3) No more wasted time reading and writing e-mails.

Frequently asked questions for Etch-A-Sketch Technical Support:

Q: My Etch-A-Sketch has all of these funny little lines all over the
screen. What should I do?

A: Pick it up and shake it.

Q: How do I turn my Etch-A-Sketch off?

A: Pick it up and shake it.

Q: What's the shortcut for Undo?

A: Pick it up and shake it.

Q: How do I create a New Document Window?

A: Pick it up and shake it.

Q: How do I set the background and foreground to the same color?

A: Pick it up and shake it.

Q: What is the proper procedure for rebooting my Etch-A-Sketch?

A: Pick it up and shake it.

Q: How do I save my Etch-A-Sketch document?

A: Don't shake it.

What a simple solution! Get rid of all computers and replace them with a worldwide network of Etch-A-Sketches! (I'm thinking about setting up an Etch-A-Sketch franchise this week.)

On the other hand . . . although the proposed solution has the upside of simplicity, it also has the downside of impracticality. It just won't work. An Etch-A-Sketch might be fun, but it cannot perform 99.99 percent of the functions computers are built to handle.

Now, you could go ahead with this plan anyway. You could allow someone to convince you to dump your computer in favor of an Etch-A-Sketch. You could even get a souped-up model with bigger dials and a bigger screen and maybe some red sand instead of the usual gray stuff. You could do that and go to bed believing that you had solved your problem.

But you would be deceived.

Take Heed...

Deception is a frequent topic throughout the Scriptures. It began as early as the Garden of Eden, but it seems to occupy an especially significant place in the prophetic passages of the New Testament. Nowhere is that more obvious than in Matthew 24, the famous "Olivet Discourse."

One day the Lord's disciples approached Jesus and asked, "Tell us, when will these things be? And what will be the sign of Your coming, and of the end of the age?" (24:3). The Master began His response with these words of warning: *"Take heed that no one deceives you."*

If ever there was a word for these times as we look toward the change of millennium, it is deception. Our Lord's warning about deception ought to be etched on our hearts. While we must always be on the alert for deception, the Lord Jesus here declares that we must be especially watchful for spiritual deceit as the day of His return approaches.

So important is this warning that it is recorded for us a second time in the Gospel of Mark: "Jesus, answering them, began to say: 'Take heed that no one deceives you. For many will come in My name, saying, "I am He," and will deceive many'" (13:5–6).

The warning is repeated yet again in Luke 21:8: "And He said: 'Take heed that you not be deceived. For many will come in My name, saying, "I am He," and, "The time has drawn near." Therefore do not go after them.'"

In these three passages, Jesus is speaking about the beginning of the tribulation period. Toward the end of the age, He warned us, there will be an increase in deception and a tremendous potential for people to be deceived. Men and women will stand up and boldly say, "I am the answer."

"Be careful," said the Lord Jesus, "that you don't run after them."

To underscore this warning, Jesus later says, "Then many false prophets will rise up and deceive many" (Matthew 24:11), and still later, "Then if anyone says to you, 'Look, here is the Christ!' or 'There!' do not believe it. For false christs and false prophets will arise and show great signs and wonders, so as to deceive, if possible, even the elect" (Matthew 24:23–24).

Three separate times in the space of twenty verses Jesus warned His disciples about the deception to come. It is as if He were saying, "Gentlemen, the primary characteristic of the days just prior to My return will be deception. You must be prepared, for the deception that's coming will be so convincing and so widespread that even My elect could be taken in by it—if such a thing were possible."

Deception in Our Day

I had never thought much about the vital importance of these warnings until I began to observe our own times more carefully. We are living in a day when men and women are being deceived right and left. In fact, one of the greatest threats to the church of Jesus Christ during these days of heightened millennial interest is deception.

Almost every week advertisements for some new system of doctrine, some new method of understanding the Bible, or some new seminar come across my desk. I read of opportunities to rear our children in "fresh" and "exciting" ways, through systems and techniques advocated by teachers with roots in churches we have known and respected for many years. And yet many times their teachings are unbiblical, dangerous, and deceptive.

This is a time when all of God's people need to keep their eyes and their Bibles wide open. We must ask God for discernment as never before.

Perhaps you're thinking, *It sounds strange to me that people who know God could be deceived.* It may sound strange, but it certainly is not unusual. Sadly, it happens all the time . . . and always has. If the danger were not so very real, why would the New Testament Epistles warn God's people about the possibility of being deceived no fewer than eleven times? (See Romans 16:18; 1 Corinthians 3:18; 6:9; 2 Corinthians 11:3; Galatians 6:7; Ephesians 5:6; Colossians 2:4; 2 Thessalonians 2:3; James 1:16, 22; 1 John 1:8.)

The history of deception in the family of God is both long and sad, beginning with the incident at the tree in the Garden of Eden. No matter how orthodox we may be, no matter how committed we are to the Word of God, no matter how much we may think we could not be vulnerable to deception, history teaches us that even faithful men and women who have named the name of almighty God have become susceptible to the deceptive tactics of the enemy. To illustrate the dangers, I would like to take you back to a period in the history of Israel when deception reigned supreme.

A Subtle Intrusion

"When Israel fell into idolatry, it did not openly renounce the worship of the God of Abraham, Isaac, and Jacob in order to bow down before the pagan shrines."[1] They did not break with the former in order to embrace the latter. Instead, a subtle intrusion into the worship of almighty God began to erode the affections and eventually the effectiveness of His people. Israel's growing policy of spiritual "tolerance" and "diversity" left the door open wide enough for deception to slip in unannounced.

When we read about the beginning of the revival that took place under Josiah, we learn how vile and perverted a worship system can become—even among God's people.

In 2 Kings 23:4 we read that King Josiah "commanded Hilkiah the high priest, the priests of the second order, and the doorkeepers, to bring out of the temple of the LORD all the articles that were made for Baal."

Were made for *whom?*

Did we read that correctly? Sadly, we did. In the temple of the living God were several articles made for the despicable Canaanite deity Baal! And not only for that pagan god, but also "for Asherah, and for all the host of heaven; and he burned them outside Jerusalem in the fields of Kidron, and carried their ashes to Bethel."

Think of it! By the time the eight-year-old Josiah became king of Judah, the worship of almighty God had become so corrupted that even in His very temple the people stored their idols of Baal and Asherah. That would be like setting up a pagan idol in front of your church and inviting people to come and burn incense to it during the week and on Sundays. Unthinkable! Abominable! And yet it happened among God's people in ancient Judah.

As the revival continued, Josiah "removed the idolatrous priests whom the kings of Judah had ordained to burn incense on the high places in the cities of Judah and in the places all around Jerusalem, and those who burned incense to Baal, to the sun, to the moon, to the constellations, and to all the host of heaven" (2 Kings 23:5).

Understand, friend. These were God's chosen people, the children of Israel. They were divinely called to worship God Almighty, but by the time Josiah came to the throne, their worship had so badly deteriorated that they had fused the worship of Yahweh with the worship of ancient Canaanite demon-gods. And it doesn't get any better as we read on.

In verses 6–7 we read, "And he brought out the wooden image from the house of the LORD, to the Brook Kidron outside Jerusalem, burned it at the Brook Kidron and ground it to ashes, and threw its ashes on the graves of the common people. Then he tore down the ritual booths of the perverted persons that were in the house of the LORD, where the women wove hangings for the wooden image." Josiah killed those who consulted mediums and spirits also (v. 24).

Remember, all of this perversion was taking place within the confines of what today we would call the church of God!

About a hundred years after these sorry events, during the ministry of Ezekiel the prophet, it happened to the people of God once more. One day the Lord gave Ezekiel a vision in which he was miraculously transported from Babylon to the inner door of the north gate of Jerusalem. There the prophet was confronted by an image set up by the wicked King Manasseh. The Bible describes it as the "the image of jealousy": "Then He said to me, 'Son of man, lift your eyes now toward the north.' So I lifted my eyes toward the north, and there, north of the altar gate, was this image of jealousy in the entrance" (Ezekiel 8:5).

This vile image was supposed to picture the Syrian mother goddess Asherah—and it was right there among the people of God, within the confines of the worship center dedicated to the Holy One of Israel. In fact, in two separate places in the temple of God, pagan idols had been set up for public worship.

And that was not the worst of it! Ezekiel tells us he was next brought to the door of the court, where he "went in and saw, and there—every sort of creeping thing, abominable beasts, and all the idols of the house of Israel, portrayed all around on the walls" (v. 10).

The people of the one true God had painted murals on the walls of the temple in honor of all the beasts and gods worshiped by their Canaanite neighbors. And Ezekiel saw yet another astonishing sight: Jewish women seated there weeping for Tammuz, another pagan god. Now remember, this was not happening in some tent out in the desert, but *in the very confines of the temple of God.*

Think of it! In God's holy city, indeed, in His holy temple, His chosen people groveled before the statue of a false god. Within mere yards of His presence in the Most Holy Place behind the veil, worshipers offered incense to images of creeping things, wept for the Babylonian nature god, and turned their backs toward the temple of the Lord in order to worship the sun to the east.

What did God think of all this? We don't have to imagine. In verse 18 He says, "Therefore I also will act in fury. My eye will not spare nor will I have pity; and though they cry in My ears with a loud voice, I will not hear them."

Commentator Herbert Schlossberg's observations are appropriate both for Ezekiel's day and our own. He said,

> In turning away from God, the nation had not fallen into irreligion, but had combined the temple religion with the pagan beliefs and practices of the surrounding people. The worship of the God of the Exodus had been defiled by merging it with the worship of the god of idols. When judgment came to the nation, it did not fall on them because they turned their back totally upon God, but because they were deceived into believing he would share his glory with any other.[2]

That is the subtle nature of deception.

Yet the people had been warned against this very turn of events! When the Israelites were about to enter the land of Canaan, God clearly and sternly told them that if they were not careful as they occupied this new world, they would be poured into a pagan mold rather than being the redemptive influence upon the world that He intended.[3]

> And it shall be, when the LORD your God brings you into the land of which He swore to your fathers, to Abraham, Isaac, and Jacob, to give you large and beautiful cities which you did not build, houses full of all good things, which you did not fill, hewn-out wells which you did not dig, vineyards and olive trees which you did not plant—when you have eaten and are full—then beware, lest you forget the LORD who brought you out of the land of Egypt, from the house of bondage. You shall fear the LORD your God and serve Him, and shall take oaths in His name. You shall not go after other gods, the gods of the peoples who are all around you (for the LORD your God is a jealous God among you), lest the anger of the LORD your God be aroused against you and destroy you from the face of the earth. (Deuteronomy 6:10–15)

Can the people of God be deceived? Yes. Are they immune from demonic deceptions that would turn their hearts away from the one true God? No. That is why we must remain vigilant. That is why we must be on our guards, "because [our] adversary the devil, as a roaring lion, walketh about, seeking whom he may devour" (1 Peter 5:8 KJV). It happened in ancient Israel, and—don't kid yourself—it can happen in the contemporary church, which is precisely why Jesus warned us about it.

Deception in the Church

As we move toward the end of the twentieth century, even the most optimistic observers express concern about the spiritual direction of our nation and of God's people within the nation. The symptoms of decay can be found in countless places . . . even where we might not think to look.

In the name of "tolerance," today's church believes it must call God both "he" and "she" and that it must describe the mother of Jesus as a "young woman" rather than as the Virgin Mary. In the name of Christianity, groups such as the Jesus Seminar attack some of the faith's most sacred doctrines. According to the scholars of the Jesus Seminar, Jesus never claimed to be the Messiah. He did not predict the end of the world. The Lord's Prayer was drawn up by Christians after Jesus died and most of the Gospels tell us nothing of the real Jesus.[4] And on and on it goes. Little by little, seductively, Satan sows his demonic seeds of deception and evil.

You say, "That will never happen in my church. We won't let it happen." My friend, the very thought that it "could never happen to us" is the first step toward our seduction. We need to keep our eyes wide open to the events happening around us. It seems that every week I get something through the mail or via the Internet that promises to help the church . . . but that contains seeds of satanic deception. No matter who endorses the product, I have learned we can never assume that it is okay.

We must remain vigilant and thoroughly evaluate new materials to ensure that they will not move people away from the core truths of God's Word. Deception has always been the weapon of choice of our enemy, and we ought to ask God during these volatile days to enable us to hear our Lord's warnings that we not be deceived.

So what can we do? How can we prepare for the battle ahead? What steps can we take to make sure we avoid "the snare of the devil" and are not "taken captive by him at his will" (2 Timothy 2:26 KJV)? I think we must begin by getting our minds ready for the onslaught to come.

Three Crucial Truths

To effectively confront these tumultuous days, we need to remind ourselves of three crucial truths. Each of us who calls himself or herself a Christian, every one of us who believes the Word of God, must move through life with a trio of biblical certainties in view.

1. The Person Behind These Deceptions Is Satan

The deception Jesus warned about and the deception we see around us aren't mere happenstance. There is a "someone" behind these deceptions, and that someone is none other than Satan, the evil enemy of our souls. He is the father of lies, and since the very beginning one of his primary weapons has been deceit. He came to Eve in the garden as the serpent, the subtle, smooth-talking deceiver.

Revelation 12:9 speaks of him as "that serpent of old, called the Devil and Satan, who deceives the whole world." And John 8:44 tells us that "There is no truth in him. . . . For he is a liar and the father of it." However Satan advertises himself, his main weapon is deception. He is a liar. He is the serpent. He is the deceiver. But he masquerades as something other than that. This pretending-to-be-something-he-isn't lies at the core of his deadly strategy.

Second Corinthians 11:13–14 says, "For such are false apostles, deceitful workers, transforming themselves into apostles of Christ. And no wonder! For Satan himself transforms himself into an angel of light."

Of course, Satan isn't always easy to identify. He's *good* at deception and he's had a lot of practice at it. But if we are to effectively heed the warnings Jesus gave us in His Olivet Discourse, we must first understand that Satan himself, the enemy of our souls, is at the bottom of all the spiritual deception in the world. My friend David Breese captures the subtlety of our adversary:

> . . . We do well to remember that the cleverest liar makes statements that sound most nearly like the truth. . . . The most subtle created being in the universe is Lucifer. The cleverest set of lies that he has ever produced is the satanic system of doctrine. With his doctrines, he presses quiet arguments upon reasonable men, appealing to the high intelligence and mature sensibilities.[5]

We need to understand that the devil is the wellspring of all lies—including those spread at the turn of the millennium.

2. The Principles of Deception Have Not Changed

Satan has one proven strategy that he has used from the beginning. He doesn't have a new playbook and he doesn't need one. Yet the unfortunate fact is that most of God's people have never analyzed his strategy. That's why they don't recognize error when it comes toward them in any of the false doctrines running rampant today.

If we want to dissect Satan's strategy, the best way to do it is to return to the place where it was first on display, in the third chapter of Genesis. Let's see if we can identify Satan's master plan and how it applies to what goes on today.

Genesis 3:1 says, "Now the serpent was more cunning than any beast of the field which the LORD God had made. And he said to the woman, 'Has God indeed said, "You shall not eat of every tree of the garden"?'"

Dispute God's Word. The first thing Satan did when he tempted Eve was to dispute God's Word. He immediately began to water down what God had said, to change it—just a little. He suggested to Eve that she may not have heard God correctly. In subtle ways he slyly disputed God's Word.

One of the ways that happens today goes something like this: You have the clear, plain Word of God in front of you, and it tells you that you shouldn't do something you'd really like to do. Next thing you know, someone sidles up alongside you and tries to give you an "alternate interpretation" of the text that will allow you to do what you know God doesn't want you to do. And so you end up saying, "I'm not sure I know what this Scripture means."

My son, Daniel, attends a secular university. He told me recently that in one of his classes, the cynical professor spent the whole class period telling his students that the Word of God is really not inspired and that it shouldn't be taken at face value. He insisted it was a book full of general guidelines intended for life in an ancient culture that no longer exists. He claimed the Bible has lost its meaning because the times have changed and that it no longer holds any meaning for modern men and women.

The class began discussing the issue of submission. Feminists in the class were standing up and taking the position that the Word of God was outdated. Daniel stood up, too, to express his confidence in the Bible, but he told me, "Dad, I can't outshout all of 'em. They just go after the Word of God."

Their aim, of course, is to chip away at the authority of the Scriptures. That has always been Satan's strategy, to undermine God's Word. He continues to say today, as he said to Eve, "You don't understand. This prohibition simply can't be real. You're a modern, intelligent woman. Do you really think a loving God would say such a thing? Really?"

Satan's first strategy is to dispute God's Word but some who have studied this text believe that his initial strategy was even more sinister. That he was

> ". . . actually making the suggestion that would amount to, 'Isn't God really saying that you cannot eat of any of the fruit of the garden?' . . . What a clever ploy! . . . The implication is that God filled the garden with a delightful array of delicious fruits to taunt man, forbidding him to eat any of these fruits. God is therefore a negativist who made man merely to frustrate him."[6]

Second, after Satan disputed God's Word, he stepped up his attack an additional notch.

Deny God's Word. "The serpent said to the woman, 'You will not surely die'" (Genesis 3:4).

The road from doubt to denial is very short. When Satan said, "You will not surely die" (3:4), it was a flat contradiction of what God had said: "But of the tree of the knowledge of good and evil you shall not eat, for in the day that you eat of it you shall surely die" (Genesis 2:17).

It is important to note the sequence here. Doubt opens the door to denial. If Eve had not listened to Satan in the beginning, she would not have been victimized in the end.

I am learning that every time you try to find an interpretation of a Scripture that will permit you to do something you know is wrong—every time you give a little ground to the devil and lose some ground from the Word of God—it isn't long until Satan drives a truck through that opening and dumps a load of stinking garbage in your life.

But he's not finished.

Displace God's Word. After he disputes God's Word and then denies it, finally he immediately moves to displacing it. He told Eve, "You will be like God" (Genesis 3:5).

Satan was putting into Eve's mind the same daring thought that had once entered his own mind and had transformed him from the anointed cherub to the devil. Warren Wiersbe warns that this strategy of the enemy continues to be successful as we approach the dawn of the millennium:

Satan's lie "You will be like God" motivates and controls much of our civilization today. Man is seeking to pull himself up by his own bootstraps. He is working to build a utopia on earth. . . . Through education, psychiatry, religions of one kind or another, and better environment, men are defying God and deifying themselves. They are playing right into the hands of Satan.[7]

That is the master strategy of Satan. He first disputes, then denies, then displaces the Word of God. One of the easiest places to see his plan at work in the world today is to observe how our culture treats sin. In the minds of many people, an "improper relationship" is different from adultery. But that's just doublespeak. In the Word of God, adultery is adultery. And when we allow Satan to sow doubt in our minds that some sin we are contemplating isn't really sin after all, we have opened our hearts to the devil's deception.

Little by little the idea of absolute truth is being eroded out of our culture. In fact, most people today no longer believe anything like absolute truth even exists. Everything is relative. Satan has so consistently and effectively sown doubt about the Word of God that, even among major congregations, the authority of the Bible has been eroded until it exerts little to no power in the lives of churchgoers.

Why have we allowed this to happen? Why have we let Satan so water down our commitment to the Word of God that we hear ourselves making statements about what is happening in our culture today that were unimaginable even ten years ago? That's Satan's master plan, and it works—as long as we let it.

And that's the key. We don't have to let Satan have control of our lives. The Apostle Paul's promise to the Corinthian Christians is still valid for twenty-first century believers: "No temptation has overtaken you except such as is common to man; but God is faithful, who will not allow you to be tempted beyond what you are able, but with the temptation will also make the way of escape, that you may be able to bear it" (1 Corinthians 10:13).

So then why do we allow Satan's master strategy to trap us? Watch carefully what Eve did, and we'll see how we fall into the same snare. Jesus told us, "Let no one deceive you," and this is how we allow ourselves to be deceived.

First, we *discount God's goodness.* Genesis 2:16 tells us, "The LORD God commanded the man, saying, 'Of every tree of the garden you may freely eat.'" But note how Eve quotes this statement in Genesis 3:2: "And the woman said to the serpent, 'We may eat the fruit of the trees of the garden.'" What did she leave out? She left out God's wonderful promise. She omitted God's gracious provision that she and Adam could *"freely"* eat of every tree in the Garden. In other words, her comprehension of God's provision was not nearly as magnanimous as God intended it to be. Satan had gotten to her with his evil implication about God.

You know, when you start to question or forget the grace and goodness of God, you begin walking down the road toward satanic deception. Ask yourself, *Is God good? Has He been good to us? Does His Word light the path ahead of us? Are His grace and provision sufficient for all our needs? In fact, hasn't He filled our cup to overflowing?*

But Satan comes along and says, "Yeah, I suppose. But if you weren't locked into that way of life, you could do this and this and that. God really isn't looking out for you; isn't it obvious? How could He want you to be alone—*again*—tonight?" And the next thing you know, he has sown his seeds of deception in your heart.

Second, Eve not only discounted God's goodness, she *dramatized God's restrictions.* Nowhere do we find that God told her or Adam not to "touch" the forbidden tree. But Eve said to the serpent, "We may eat the fruit of the trees of the garden; but of the fruit of the tree which is in the midst of the garden, God has said, 'You shall not eat it, nor shall you touch it, lest you die'" (Genesis 3:2–3).

But God never said that. He made no mention of "touching."

What difference does that make? Good question. I think the answer is that when you give Satan an inroad into your life, you'll soon be thinking less of the grace of God and more of the law of God. And the next thing you know you begin to think that God doesn't really care about you. Maybe He isn't interested in your welfare at all.

That is how deception gets into our lives. Almost every week of my life as a pastor, I've seen that demonic process played out. Young people and older people. New Christians and individuals who have been in the church for years. The rich and the poor. The highly educated and grade school dropouts. Pastors and deacons and trustees who begin to argue about God's grace, who equivocate about whether the times are really the same as when the Word of God was written—and shouldn't they be allowed a little more freedom in today's culture?

Eve discounted God's goodness, she dramatized God's restrictions, and finally she *diminished God's penalty.* She said, "lest you die." But that's not what God said. In Genesis 2:17 the Lord declared, "But of the tree of the knowledge of good and evil you shall not eat, for in the day that you eat of it you shall surely die." Eve left out the "surely die" part and changed it to a simple "lest you die."

When put like that, the penalty for disobedience does not seem so certain. And once you look at the Word of God in this fashion, you leave yourself wide open to the deception of Satan.

It's the same today. Satan comes to our young people and whispers seductively, "You know, you've got all of these drives within you. God put them there. He surely never meant for you to be frustrated all the time. After all, everybody's doing it. We live in a sexually free environment, and yeah, I know you're a Christian—but *good night!* You're also human. God expects you to be happy."

And the next thing you know, the young Christian finds himself or herself in a compromising situation, with a load of regret pressing down with the weight of the world. That young person would give anything to just go back and reverse what Satan deceived him or her into doing. But it's too late.

Listen, the devil doesn't want to help anyone! He wants to destroy, not build. He wants to enslave, not liberate. Remember, he "walks about like a roaring lion, seeking whom he may devour." Of course, he never does it in an obvious or obnoxious way. He does it deceptively, by sowing little seeds of doubt about the Word of God. As David Breese observes:

> Satan moves in the lives of people from a lesser degree to the greater. He began his assault by establishing a small beachhead and moves from this point of moral fault into a program of larger conquest. He ultimately intends to consume us, but this devouring begins with the smallest nibble. He conceals his objectives, making it appear that he is devoted to our happiness.[8]

As we move toward the new millennium, that is the most critical thing we as God's people need to understand. Satan has begun a rampage of deceptions running around under many stripes, and if we are not aware of it, we will be victimized by it.

3. The Power Over Deception Is Jesus Christ

Against the backdrop of Satan's deceit stands Jesus Christ, the personification of truth. Our Lord said of Himself, "I am the way, the truth, and the life. No one comes to the Father except through Me" (John 14:6). How important it is for believers to understand that Jesus Christ is the champion of truth. When we follow Him, we walk in the truth and we are not deceived by the many false prophets who have gone out into the world (1 John 4:1). When "... we are of God. He who knows God hears us; he who is not of God does not hear us. By this we know the spirit of truth and the spirit of error." (1 John 4:6).

If we stay with the truth, Satan can't get in. When we saturate our minds and hearts with God's truth and we live in the truth, we will be set free and deception can't manhandle us. But when we play with the deceptive words of Satan and allow that deception into our hearts, we open the door for him to wreak havoc in our lives and in the lives of our families. Every ruined family that I know of started with the deceptive lie of Satan, whispered in the ear of a man or woman, that "it's all right if you really feel good about it and you don't think anybody else will find out."

Every time God's people suffer destruction it is because the deceiver has been allowed just a little foothold in the door. My friend, be ruthless against that! When you see that foot edging in the doorway, be pitiless in the way you deal with it. How pitiless? The Bible says we are to "crucify" it. Crucifixion hurts! It's an agonizing, bloody business. But it's also permanent. And that's the kind of response we must make every time we see the devil's foot near the doorjamb. Crucify those impulses with pitiless abandon and do not allow the enemy even a tiny advantage in your life.

Shine Like Stars

Of what use is the study of prophecy? Why should you listen to Jesus about what lies ahead in the future? For one thing, it will keep you from tripping over the deception of the enemy and falling into his deadly snares.

Everything we have considered in this chapter is prophetic truth. The one who started this deception in the Garden continued his deceit in the land of Israel and has remained busy throughout the days of the church. Jesus tells us that he will be given free rein for a little while at the end of this age, assisted by a brilliant, wicked man the Bible calls "the man of sin" or "the Antichrist."

Antichrist will be the embodiment of everything Satan ever wanted in this life. He will be the deceiver of all human deceivers, and the Bible says his deception will be so powerful that, if it were possible, he would deceive even the elect.

That's where this long road of satanic deception is headed, and we are even now merging onto that broad highway. As we move toward the end of the age, as we move toward the time when the Lord Jesus comes back, we will see increasingly more of this deception. First Timothy 4:1 plainly tells us that this deception will grow: "The Spirit expressly says that in latter times some will depart from the faith, giving heed to deceiving spirits and doctrines of demons."

I believe we are living on the edge of the latter times. Already the spirit of deception is rampant among us. But let us not forget that in the midst of the problem, there is Jesus! In the midst of the deception, there is the living, victorious, eternal Truth. In the midst of the great seduction of our times, there is the absolute, rock-solid person of the Lord Jesus Christ, the One Who is the Way, the Truth, and the Life.

When you put your trust fully in Him, when you make His Word your sourcebook, you can live above deception. You can live on the level of truth and God will honor you. You can be a shining light in the midst of the gathering darkness of this age.

In fact, you have a choice to make. God says you can be one of two kinds of stars. You can be like the ones described in the book of Jude: "Wandering stars, to whom is reserved the blackness of darkness for ever" (Jude 13 KJV); or you can choose a considerably brighter future and become the kind of star Paul describes in Philippians 2:15–16: "children of God without fault in a crooked and depraved generation, in which you shine like stars in the universe as you hold out the word of life" (NIV).

Even if you don't know a lot about prophecy, this choice is a no-brainer. I don't need a computer to assist me—or even an Etch-A-Sketch.

I'll stake my future on the Word of Life.

Three

DO NOT BE TROUBLED

These are days when fear rides the headlines. Even sitting in a dentist's waiting room, you cannot easily avoid newspaper or magazine articles reporting the great and daunting challenges our world faces as we spin our way through time and space into an uncertain future.

A Russian meltdown?

A year 2000 disaster?

A worldwide recession?

A loss of national sovereignty to global agencies?

A superstrain of killer viruses resistant to all known antibiotics?

How do we respond to such a barrage of negative, often frightening articles and predictions? Actually, we might take one of several approaches.

There's the proverbial ostrich approach: We can stick our heads in the sand and ignore it all. Some people love to live in ignorance. They have little knowledge about the problems facing our nation and world, and they really don't *want* such knowledge. They prefer the false security of earplugs and blinders. "Nothing can trouble me; nothing can hurt me," they say, "because I don't pay attention to upsetting things."

Then there's the "so what?" approach. With a quick, noncommittal shrug of the shoulders, we say, "Oh, I suppose we'll muddle through it somehow, just like we always have. Anyway, what can I do about it? Just as long as my investments are doing well, my satellite dish pulls in two hundred channels, and I'm able to make my car payments, I'll get along." These folks go through life humming the old hit from the fifties, *"Qué será será, whatever will be, will be."*

Others, however, reject both of these approaches, recognizing that we really must think seriously about the crucial issues facing our culture today—whether we want to or not. What kinds of issues? In the most recent report of the National Center for Victims of Crime, the following statistics provide the answer.

> In 1997 there was a violent crime every 19 seconds. . . . The number of child victims increased by 118% (1996). . . . There were 307,000 attempted or completed rapes and sexual assaults, 1,134,000 attempted or completed robberies, 7,683,000 attempted or completed assaults and 27.3 million property crimes. . . . Fraud causes an estimated monetary loss of 40 billion annually for victims of personal fraud commonly involving deception and abuse of trust for financial gain. . . . Domestic violence kills 58,000 people every five years, the same number lost in the Vietnam War.[1]

Add to those grim statistics the cruel and murderous way in which we deal with unborn infants, and you can readily see that our country has profound problems. Deep stress fractures run through the very foundation blocks of our culture.

As we contemplate these situations, we might be tempted toward fatalism. We might throw our hands in the air and say, "What's the use? We're headed for hades in a handbasket. We're Sodom and Gomorrah on the way to the fire. Let's just move to some cave in the Ozarks and wait for the end."

What do you and I really need in these troubling days? We don't need a hideout in the hills. We don't need a backdoor fire escape. We don't need more entertainment to dull our senses and divert our energies. We don't need to allow accumulated anxiety and dread to push us into a heart attack or ulcers.

What we need is perspective. And while that commodity may be in short supply in our uptight world, it is the very heartbeat of God's Word. Perspective flows from the pages of Scripture like water from an artesian well. As our Lord walked this earth and taught in the streets and the synagogues and across the hills and valleys of Palestine, perspective filled His words. No one ever spoke like this Man. He had a way of continually amazing even those closest to Him, which is exactly what happened when His disciples came to Him with three troubling questions about the future.

A Prophecy

Do you have a favorite place near your home where you can view the surrounding area? Maybe it's a hill that overlooks your town or some vista point where you can gaze for miles out across the countryside. If you live in a prairie state like Kansas, you may have to remember a time when you visited Colorado and looked back from some scenic vantage point in the foothills of the Rockies at the wide sweep of the Great Plains stretching to the horizon. It's either that or climb a water tower!

Can you imagine walking such a trail with the Lord Jesus Christ? Can you picture yourself finding a grassy spot and sitting down with Him there in the mellow light of an autumn afternoon? What sorts of questions would you ask Him if you were free to ask Him about anything? I think I would want to ask Him about the future. I would look out to that distant, hazy horizon and ask Him what lies ahead in the coming weeks and months.

That's just what His disciples did as they sat together on the slope of the Mount of Olives. All the way up that hill, these men had been puzzling over a remark Jesus had made as they left the temple area in the city.

> Then Jesus went out and departed from the temple, and His disciples came to Him to show Him the buildings of the temple. And Jesus said to them, "Do you not see all these things? Assuredly, I say to you, not one stone shall be left here upon another, that shall not be thrown down." Now as He sat on the Mount of Olives, the disciples came to Him privately, saying, "Tell us, when will these things be? And what will be the sign of Your coming, and of the end of the age?" And Jesus answered and said to them: "Take heed that no one deceives you. For many will come in My name, saying, 'I am the Christ,' and will deceive many. And you will hear of wars and rumors of wars. See that you are not troubled; for all these things must come to pass, but the end is not yet." (Matthew 24:1–6)

When the disciples heard Jesus' teaching concerning the temple, they assumed He was speaking of the end times. Like many Jews of that era, they were looking and longing for a Messiah to bring political, rather than spiritual, leadership. They wanted Christ to set up His throne and His kingdom, and as far as they were concerned, it couldn't happen fast enough. More than anything, they wanted the Roman gentiles thrown out of their nation and the holy city.

The disciples' first question was *When?* "When will these things be?" Meticulous Dr. Luke captured the Lord's answer in greatest detail in Luke 21. Jesus gave the disciples both specific information and some concrete things to watch for in the days to come. The second question was *What?* "What will be the sign of Your coming?"

And the third question was another *What?* "What will be the signs of the end of the age?"

In Matthew 24, Jesus takes the time to answer these questions in detail. As He unfolds these truths, He gives His disciples three things to watch for—three signs of His imminent return.

Now, you have to understand that Matthew 24 primarily addresses what we call the Second Advent—that climactic moment when the Son of God returns to earth with power and great glory to judge the nations. That event takes place after the rapture of the church, after the earth has passed through the Great Tribulation. While Jesus does not speak directly to the Rapture in this passage, His words roll back the fog that shrouds great and momentous events. He shows us just how world circumstances will begin to shape themselves as the time of His coming draws near. And the very first sign He mentions is one we noted in the previous chapter.

1. The Sign of Deception

Jesus warned of a great increase in deception. He urged His people not to be swayed or seduced by false messiahs and antichrists.

The spirit of antichrist runs rampant through our world. Satan never seems to run out of counterfeits; hell's warehouses are stocked to the rafters with them. Everywhere you turn, you hear and read people's wild proclamations about the future. As I write these words, newspaper headlines speak of a Denver-based "doomsday" cult rounded up and shipped home by Israeli security agents. According to Israel, the group is plotting bloody violence at the turning of the millennium. For what reason? To hasten the Apocalypse and the second coming of Jesus.

As if heaven needs assistance to draw this age to a close!

Jesus warned that as we move toward the end of the age, deceptions such as these will multiply. At the same time, He reminded His disciples that disputes among nations will escalate dramatically.

2. The Sign of Disputes Among Nations

Jesus warned the disciples they would hear of wars and rumors of wars. He explained that nation would rise against nation, and kingdom against kingdom. Jesus said we should understand the escalation of wars and dissension among groups of people as a clear signal of His forthcoming return to earth.

At this writing, though conflicts smolder and rumble across our globe, our own nation lives in a time of relative peace. Most of us find ourselves hoping that "no one gets careless," but we cannot dodge the biblical fact that wars and disputes among nations will escalate as the world winds down to judgment.

3. The Sign of Devastation

Christ warned there would be famines and pestilences and earthquakes in various places. We cannot turn on the television today without seeing somebody trying to raise money to feed the hungry. Displaced by war and weather, millions across our world will go to bed hungry tonight. And as we draw closer to the end time, Jesus declared that these tragic conditions will continuously escalate.

And earthquakes? They are often on the minds of folks here in southern California. In the tenth century, there were 32 earthquakes. In the fifteenth century, 147. In the seventeenth century, there were 378. But in the nineteenth century, there were 2,119 earthquakes. There has been just as drastic an increase in intensity as there has been in frequency. Ten of the thirteen most devastating earthquakes of all time have occurred in the twentieth century. Of some 68 major earthquakes recorded in history, 46 have occurred in our century.[2]

When Jesus spoke of devastations, however, He had more than earthquakes in mind. Plagues like AIDS and other deadly new viruses now race across the globe. In the United States, 350,000 have died since the epidemic began. Each year, 40,000 are infected. And a total of 650,000 to 900,000 are believed to be infected with HIV.[3] All of these are signs that the time of Christ's return grows nearer.

But what does the Lord Jesus say about all this? What's His commentary on today's worrisome headlines? "See that you are not troubled; for all these things must come to pass" (Matthew 24:6).

What? *Not troubled?* Are you kidding? What do You mean, Lord? How could we keep from being alarmed and troubled by all the terrors and devastations visiting our planet?

Listen to it again: "And Jesus answered and said to them . . . 'You will hear of wars and rumors of wars. See that you are not troubled.'" Why? "For all these things must come to pass, but the end is not yet" (Matthew 24:4–6).

Jesus was telling His disciples that these rumblings and shakings signal the beginning of the end. The end is not yet—but it's in sight. Day by day, it is drawing closer.

Have you ever driven along a high mountain pass and noticed those big warning signs for trucks? A bright yellow sign declares: *First Warning. 6% Downgrade Ahead.* That's plenty steep—especially for a fully loaded semi. That sign would be enough to make most any truckdriver sit up a little straighter in his cab. You go a little farther and another sign repeats the message: *Second Warning. 6% Downgrade Ahead. Trucks Check Brakes.* Not long after that you see a sign that says: *Runaway Truck Ramp Five Miles Ahead.*

You haven't started downhill yet; the terrain is still level. But you've encountered warning after warning that the road ahead plunges steeply. Truckers with too heavy loads or faulty brakes will be in grave danger if they ignore those signs and roar on down the highway. Once they go over the crest, there may be no turning back.

That's what these warnings of our Lord accomplish. They tell us, "Things may seem smooth and even now, but watch out! You're moving toward the edge. You're approaching a stretch of highway radically different from the one you're traveling right now."

Those of us who have put our trust in Jesus Christ as Savior and Lord know that before these things become full-blown, He will take us right out of this world to be with Himself. The Word of God tells us that those who belong to Him will never see these devastations and sorrow in their ultimate form.

A Parable

Great future events cast long shadows.

These cataclysmic end-time occurrences won't happen in just a day. A gradual buildup to these terminal episodes unfolds over the months and years. I believe we're in the midst of that building-up phase at this very moment.

Jesus told a parable to help His disciples understand this process: "Now learn this parable from the fig tree: When its branch has already become tender and puts forth leaves, you know that summer is near. So you also, when you see all these things, know that it is near, at the very doors" (Matthew 24:32–33).

When the disciples asked Jesus about His return, He gave them some details, then also spoke this little parable to help them understand how all the pieces fit together. Our Lord was the greatest storyteller of His time, so we shouldn't be surprised that He used a vivid word picture to drive home His point.

Jesus encourages us to learn from the fig tree. When its branch becomes tender and puts forth its leaves, we know that summer is on the way. If the Lord had chosen to live in another part of the world, He might have said, "When you see those little crocus flowers pushing their blossoms up through the snow, you know that spring is just around the corner." The Lord's word picture serves as a window, enabling us to gaze through to the truth. It helps us to understand that when certain signs emerge right in front of our eyes, we can nod our heads and say, "Yes, that's just as the Lord said it would be. The time of His coming must be very near."

Watch those yellow warning signs, He is telling us. The road will change up ahead, and there is no reason to be taken by surprise. It's time to wake up and understand that things are not going to continue as they always have. Harvest isn't here yet . . . but it's one day closer than ever before.

The Lord was probably walking by a fig tree when He pointed at its branches, using the tree as an illustration of His coming. The apostle Paul employed an even more graphic picture—and one that may have special significance to many women readers of this book. The insightful apostle used the illustration with a group of believers in Thessalonica:

"For when they say, 'Peace and safety!' then sudden destruction comes upon them, as labor pains upon a pregnant woman. And they shall not escape" (1 Thessalonians 5:3).

The primary signs of the Lord's coming, Paul tells us, are like labor pains. At first, the pains aren't intense at all. I'm told these initial stirrings are really more uncomfortable than painful. A woman may feel one such pang, and then not feel another for twenty minutes or more. But as birth approaches (as some of you might readily attest!) the pain gets a little more intense—and the pains get closer together. And when you reach a stage where the pain is very intense—and those pains are gripping you with regular frequency—you know you'd better get to the hospital, or you'll be giving birth in the backseat of the car.

The pain grows.

The intensity grows.

The frequency grows.

And then . . . life changes.

That, I believe, is how we should look at the signs of the Second Coming. As we see those manifestations grow sharper and more incessant, we should understand that our redemption is drawing nigh.

A Picture

The apostle Paul adds a wonderful picture to our understanding of these events in 2 Thessalonians chapter 2. Each of the New

Testament letters—whether penned by Peter or Paul, John or Jude—explains and amplifies our Lord's teaching in the Gospels. And in this second letter to the Thessalonians, Paul paints a stunning little miniature, helping us to understand how to respond to all the bad news of our day.

As I read Paul's words, I'm intrigued to once again run into that little word *trouble*.

> Now, brethren, concerning the coming of our Lord Jesus Christ and our gathering together to Him, we ask you, not to be soon shaken in mind or troubled, either by spirit or by word or by letter, as if from us, as though the day of Christ had come. Let no one deceive you by any means. (2 Thessalonians 2:1–3)

That counsel sounds familiar, doesn't it? Don't be shaken! Don't be troubled! Keep it all in perspective!

Next Paul warns the Thessalonians concerning the false teaching that seemed to shake their equilibrium and trigger their fears. Apparently, they were being told that the Day of the Lord, or the Tribulation, had already come. No wonder they were troubled!

Have you ever had such a bad week that you thought the Tribulation had already come? This little band of believers had endured week after week, month after month of pressure, persecution, and anxiety because of their faith in Christ. And then, as if that weren't trouble enough, someone came along with a seminar, a paperback book, and a videotape telling them that the end was already upon them. The deceptive message ran something like this: "I know that you heard that the Tribulation was in the future, but it is not in the future. It is now."

Some of these false teachers even went so far as to sign Paul's name at the end of their letters. They claimed to speak in the apostle's name and authority. How distressing those forgeries and deceptions must have been to this godly missionary and shepherd! (If you've ever been misrepresented by an enemy, you know how deep that pain can be.) With a sense of great urgency, Paul wrote to the believers, urging them to reject these deceptive teachings. In fact, when you get to the end of this letter, in 2 Thessalonians 3:17, the apostle deliberately pens these final words: "I, Paul, write this greeting in my own hand, which is the distinguishing mark in all my letters. This is how I write" (NIV).

In other words, "This is my letter, and this is my signature. Whatever recent letters you think you received from me saying the Tribulation has already come are fakes and forgeries. Don't be taken in!"

In his first letter to the Thessalonians, Paul had already taught these believers that the Tribulation was future—and that they would escape it. Listen to the assurance ringing in these words from his first letter:

> For they themselves report what kind of reception you gave us. They tell how you turned to God from idols to serve the living and true God, and to wait for his Son from heaven, whom he raised from the dead—Jesus, *who rescues us from the coming wrath.* (1 Thessalonians 1:9–10 NIV, emphasis added*)*

The Thessalonians had been clearly taught that Jesus would return and deliver them from the end-time wrath. But now someone had sent them a message saying, "That's all wrong. The Tribulation is already here—and you're in the middle of it."

By the way, there are many folks sending such messages these days. I get them almost every week in my mailbox. Some are so vociferous they go out of their way to discredit every Bible teacher who teaches otherwise. You wouldn't believe how vicious their statements and accusations can be.

Later on in 1 Thessalonians 5:9, we have the same truth again: "For God did not appoint us to wrath, but to obtain salvation through our Lord Jesus Christ." I have people tell me all the time that this "wrath" has nothing to do with the Tribulation. If you believe that, you have not read the book of Revelation! You should go back and read chapters 5 through 19 where John specifically talks about God's wrath upon this earth.

The Bible teaches that when we are saved, when we trust Christ, we are no longer under the judgment of God. "If anyone is in Christ, he is a new creation; old things have passed away; behold, all things have become new"; "There is therefore now no condemnation to those who are in Christ Jesus" (2 Corinthians 5:17; Romans 8:1).

Some say the "condemnation" of Romans 8:1 applies only to sin. But that's not what the passage states. It says: "*no* condemnation." God will not judge His people whom He sent His Son to save. The white-hot fury of His wrath was already poured out upon Jesus Christ on the cross, and that judgment was full and complete. He will not again judge us as His people. The Bridegroom will not permit His bride to suffer the wrath He already endured for her. He will rather take us to glory to be with Him.

The Thessalonians had been upset by pseudoscholars who claimed to have an inside track on God's agenda for the future. Like so many teachers today, they might have had charts and graphs and mathematical equations to buttress their alarmist teachings. But Paul told the believers (and I love these words), "I don't want you to be troubled."

My friend, one of the greatest ways in all the world to untrouble your heart is to get into the Word of God. When you plunge yourself into the pages of this eternal Book, your troubles are taken care of. It's like climbing that tall hill I mentioned earlier; the Word enables you to see above and beyond the gray mist and the low-lying clouds.

If you want a troubled heart, if you want confusion, anxiety, and mental paralysis, just neglect your Bible and keep listening to all those other voices filling the newspapers and airwaves. Read the magazines. Listen to talk radio. You'll find all the trouble you can handle! But when you've had enough of it, when your heart is weary and you long for perspective and rest and fresh hope, get alone with God and an open Bible. The Holy Spirit will bring illumination to your mind and peace and perspective to your soul.

I recently read a book in which the author confessed she had been reading so many commentaries on the Scriptures that she hadn't been spending much time in the Bible itself. One day she decided to push all those other books aside for a season and just immerse herself in God's Word.

I respect that lady's decision. Sometimes we need to remove every voice from our ears but the voice of the Lord God Himself. That may take a little doing! It may mean getting up an hour earlier in the morning. It may mean getting away by yourself for a while in an isolated place. It may even mean locking yourself in the bathroom! Whatever it takes, we need to hear the calming voice of our Shepherd in these troubled times.

A Perspective

Paul wanted the Thessalonians to experience the life-changing perspective of God's wisdom and God's Word. And as it turned out, Paul's timid young friend Timothy needed a strong dose of that same medicine. In the apostle's two letters to that embattled pastor, Paul sought to give Timothy a telephoto perspective on what the end times would really look like. You may never have had the opportunity to read these descriptive verses in sequence before. I think you'll find, as I did, that it makes for a very revealing picture.

1. A Rebellion

Now the Spirit expressly says that in latter times some will depart from the faith, giving heed to deceiving spirits and doctrines of demons, speaking lies in hypocrisy, having their own conscience seared with a hot iron, forbidding to marry, and commanding to abstain from foods which God created to be received with thanksgiving by those who believe and know the truth. (1 Timothy 4:1–3)

But know this, that in the last days perilous times will come: For men will be lovers of themselves, lovers of money, boasters, proud, blasphemers, disobedient to parents, unthankful, unholy, unloving, unforgiving, slanderers, without self-control, brutal, despisers of good, traitors, headstrong, haughty, lovers of pleasure rather than lovers of God, having a form of godliness but denying its power. And from such people turn away! (2 Timothy 3:1–5)

For the time will come when they will not endure sound doctrine, but according to their own desires, because they have itching ears, they will heap up for themselves teachers; and they will turn their ears away from the truth, and be turned aside to fables. (2 Timothy 4:3–4)

Listen carefully, my friend. What Paul predicted to Timothy has already happened and continues to happen!

Paul said that before the Day of the Lord would come, the church at large would turn away from the long-held truths of the faith. That is exactly what you will find in most any city or town in our nation. There has never been such a conglomerate mess in the church of Jesus Christ as there is today. Perhaps you have experienced the bewilderment of trying one church after another and encountering diluted truth mixed with the contradictory teachings of men.

And it doesn't matter what the "label" says on the outside of the church. If you don't walk through those doors with some caution and discernment, you have no idea what you're getting into. You may find New Age ideology edging out biblical truth. You may find teaching locked into "positive mental attitudes," designed to make everyone feel good all the time.

How would you like to be a newscaster who delivered only good news in every broadcast? It sounds great, except . . . it isn't real, is it? God's Word speaks to every human situation and the language isn't always festooned with hearts and flowers and smiley faces. The Bible takes on sin at its roots, just as a surgeon pursues cancer in the human body. It isn't always pleasant and it isn't always pretty—but it saves lives.

Both Jesus and Paul declared there would be a major departing from the truth in the days immediately prior to the Lord's return. The birth pangs have started, haven't they? The intensity is growing, as is the frequency. It is becoming more and more difficult to figure out what is going on, even in old, staid, established churches. In pulpits where truth used to be proclaimed with power, you now find pastors and teachers questioning both the miracles and the historicity of the Bible itself.

What's happening? We are experiencing the rebellion, the falling away. It's another big yellow sign on the road to the end times.

2. A Removal

Scripture also speaks of a removal. Look again at 2 Thessalonians 2:7: "For the mystery of lawlessness is already at work; only He who now restrains will do so until He is taken out of the way."

What is this "restraining"? It is an invisible force holding back the gathered might of ultimate evil. As bad as it is today in our world, it could (and will) get worse. A restraining influence in our world holds this evil—this dark satanic tide of perversion and lawlessness—in check. Who has the power to restrain Satan? Only God. And it is God the Holy Spirit, the third person of the Trinity, who draws the line today and keeps the ocean of evil at bay.

Paul said to the Thessalonians, "Friends, don't be troubled by these letters purporting to come from me. You are not in the midst of the Tribulation. The day of the Lord has not come, and will not come until the rebellion against the truth has reached full force, and until that restraining power that holds evil in check is finally removed."

When will that restraining influence cease? When the Holy Spirit no longer has the ministry He has now. And when will that happen? When the church is taken out of the way at the Rapture.

Let me ask you a question. Where does the Holy Spirit live? He lives within the believer. When the Rapture comes, all the believers will be swept up into heaven and the Holy Spirit will no longer have a resident ministry on this earth. His role will revert to what it was in the Old Testament. If you think conditions are dark and vile now, just try to imagine the way things will be when all the restraints are suddenly removed. It would be like immediately removing all the dikes that surround the Netherlands. Sin and death and hatred and perversion will suddenly rush in to fill the vacuum left by the departure of the church and the presence of the Spirit. When that occurs, the Great Tribulation isn't far behind.

Paul said, "I don't want you to be anxious and upset, as though these things had already happened." We are in the buildup to the rebellion. We have seen the yellow signs on the mountain pass and we know the highway ahead of us plunges into steep decline.

How soon? Who knows? The next sound you and I hear could well be the trumpet call of God. Then, before we can even take a breath or blink our eyes, we will be racing together through the stratosphere to meet the Lord in the air. Hallelujah!

3. A Revelation

The third thing Paul said would have to happen is the revelation of "the lawless one." He writes: "For the mystery of lawlessness is already at work; only He who now restrains will do so until He is taken out of the way. *And then the lawless one will be revealed,* whom the Lord will consume with the breath of His mouth and destroy with the brightness of His coming" (2 Thessalonians 2:7–8, emphasis added).

Who is this "lawless one"? It is the Antichrist. Just this past week a man called me at my office and told me he knew the identity of the Antichrist. He wanted to meet with me personally so he could "reveal" the identity. Everybody's got an idea or theory . . . and I just don't have time for most of them. Nevertheless, the Bible tells us clearly that before the Day of the Lord arrives and the Tribulation sweeps across our world, many in the church will turn away from the truth, the rapture of the church will take place, and the one called "Antichrist" will be revealed.

A Prescription

Do you see how the Word of God can help you keep your perspective?

Have you ever been in a jetliner headed home from a long trip, when you suddenly began thinking about the pilot and copilot in the cabin? How do they manage to fly that craft halfway across the continent and head straight for my hometown? How do they aim that thing through storms and clouds and dead of night and endless lonely miles and make a pinpoint landing in San Diego, on runway five?

The Scriptures are like the guidance system used by the pilot to fly thousands of miles through the dark. Our knowledge of Scripture can help us know what to say and where to go, how to plan and prepare and respond in any situation of life.

As Paul wraps up his discussion on these prophetic themes in 2 Thessalonians 2, he seems to take a deep breath and launch into a little pep talk. He tells his readers three things they should do in light of what he has taught them. These same three things can guide you and me through the growing darkness of our culture and keep us on track with a life pleasing to God.

1. Stand Fast

Notice what he says in verse 15: "Therefore, brethren, stand fast and hold the traditions which you were taught, whether by word or our epistle."

Great counsel! In other words, don't go running after some new doctrine, some exotic teaching. This is not the time to explore novel ideas about theology. If we've been instructed in the truth and know the Word of God, it's time to dig our roots down deep.

You might say, "Dr. Jeremiah, I've been experimenting a bit with some of the New Age things I've been reading about." Don't you do that! Stand fast in the truth that you know. Satan's quick foot can fit in the smallest crack of slightly opened doors. That's all the invitation he needs to build a stronghold in your life and send you down the road into obscure and destructive teachings. If there ever has been a time for you and I to be dogmatic and unequivocal about known truth, this is it.

Some will say, "But Dr. Jeremiah, that doesn't sound 'tolerant.' Aren't we supposed to show 'tolerance' these days?" Do you know how I'd answer that question? I want to be just as tolerant as God is. And God is mighty intolerant of that which is not true. So let's be as intolerant (in a sweet, Christian way) as He is.

And while you are standing fast, don't forget to . . .

2. Hold On

I love this. Paul says, "Stand fast and hold the traditions which you were taught. . . . Now may our Lord Jesus Christ Himself, and our God and Father, who has loved us and given us everlasting consolation and good hope by grace, comfort your hearts" (2 Thessalonians 2:15–17).

This is no time to be discouraged or buried under the circumstances. If reading the newspaper in the morning discourages you, stay away from it. Read the Word of God instead and save all that bad news for a time when you can prepare for it—and then recover from it. The news isn't good these days. If you think about it much, it can drag you down.

But in the midst of it all, there is Jesus.

In the midst of it all, the Shepherd offers clear-eyed perspective, speaks calmly to our hearts, and whispers words of encouragement and hope. In this particular time of our lives, as a church and as a culture, we should ask God to help us fall in love with our Savior as never before. We ought to cultivate that relationship until He is not just one thing in our life, He is THE thing in our life . . . and even life itself. He is the very focus of who we are. So stand fast. Hold on. And then one final word . . .

3. Work Hard

Now may our Lord Jesus Christ Himself, and our God and Father . . . establish you in every good word and work. (2 Thessalonians 2:16–17)

My friend, this is not a time to climb into a white robe, sit on a fence, and get a stiff neck looking up into the sky, waiting for the Lord's return. This is a time to get busy for God. Use the powers and energy and gifting He gives you. Maximize the time. Cash in on opportunities. One of the most simple objectives of a Christian is not only to go to heaven, but to take as many people with you as you can! Share the gospel, teach children, build up the weak, strengthen the faltering, encourage the fallen, and reach a strong hand to those who are hurting. In every good work, "occupy till I come," said the Lord.

The road divides up ahead and we've already seen the warning signs. It's no time to fall asleep at the wheel.

Four

DO NOT BE CONFUSED

When Jesus departed from this earth, the disciples watched Him ascend into the sky until they could no longer see Him.

But they kept looking. Squinting their eyes against the glare, they stared into the heavens, as if expecting Him to come right back down again. It finally took an angelic nudge to shake these bewildered men from their preoccupation. *The Living Bible* paraphrases Luke's account from the book of Acts:

> As they were straining their eyes for another glimpse, suddenly two white-robed men were standing there among them, and said, "Men of Galilee, why are you standing here staring at the sky? Jesus has gone away to heaven, and some day, just as he went, he will return!" (Acts 1:10–11 TLB)

Those angels had an important point to make. Jesus said He would return and He will. In the meantime, it serves no good purpose to stand around staring at the sky. There's work to do! Our faith assures us that He will return, but our *focus* must be on accomplishing the King's business until that great day arrives.

Setting dates for the Lord's return is a lot like staring into an empty sky. It does nothing at all to advance His purposes on earth and distracts from our rightful focus as believers. Beyond that, date-setting can create a great deal of harm—and even tragedy.

What Happened to the "Christian Century"?

A hundred years ago Christians in this country anticipated the greatest century the world had ever known. Technology blossomed on every hand. Henry Ford, Thomas Edison, and a host of other inventors busied themselves creating devices that would ease the path and lighten the load for millions of average Americans. Electricity began to illumine tall buildings and city streets. These were days of unbridled optimism, and the slogans arising out of this era reflected this positive spirit. You heard Christians say things such as "ever onward and upward," or "the evangelization of our world in our generation," or "the absoluteness of Christianity."

In the early days of 1900, a number of broad-minded souls launched a new journal they called *The Christian Century*. That's what these Christian journalists thought they could look forward to in those dawning days of the twentieth century: a hundred years of peace, progress, and Christianization. In those days, reminders of "the soon coming of Jesus Christ" were looked upon as lunatic-fringe talk.

Now we're at the end of that century, looking back. And oh, how different the view appears from this vantage point! It has been an era of unparalleled brutality and moral meltdown.[1] It might even be said that it has been the most un-Christian century since Jesus walked on earth. We are, as Timothy George has written:

Awash in a sea of apocalypticism . . . end-times hysteria rules the airwaves and repeatedly surfaces as a distinctive feature [in] such bizarre and deadly tragedies as the Branch Davidian killings in Waco, the subway attack in Tokyo, and the recent carnage in Oklahoma City.[2]

If you listened to reports of any of those events, you heard someone, even secular newscasters, somehow connect them to talk of the millennium before us.

We know that our Lord will return; we have taken note of the signs He listed for us and believe His return is imminent. Yet to invest time and energy and focus in seeking to set a specific date for that event is not only unwise, but a gross violation of Scripture.

Date setters, of course, have been with us for centuries. In the second century, a group of Montanists were convinced that Jesus would come back to Phrygia, a region of Asia Minor.

More recently, in 1983, Mary Stewart Relfe wrote that she had been praying to know the year of the Lord's coming. As a result of those prayers, she now knew that World War III was just ahead—which would result in the partial destruction of the United States by nuclear attack. "It was," she wrote, "one of the most tremendous divine revelations I have ever received from the Lord." So specific was that "vision" that she produced a chart showing how World War III would commence in 1989, with the Great Tribulation following in 1990. According to the chart, Jesus Christ Himself would return to earth in 1997.[3]

Apparently, someone forgot to fax the Lord a copy of that chart.

Reginald Dunlop, a California author of numerous self-published books, prophesied worldwide famine by 1986 resulting in enormous death tolls. The United States itself, he asserted, would feel hunger pains for the first time. It would be so bad, he insisted, that human body parts would be sold in stores throughout the nation.[4]

Lester Sumrall, a founder of the LeSEA Broadcasting Company, set his sights (along with many others) on the year 2000. He wrote: "I predict the absolute fullness of man's operation on planet Earth by the year 2000 A.D. Then Jesus Christ will reign from Jerusalem for a thousand years."[5]

Sumrall wasn't alone in his dire predictions for the year 2000. Apocalypticists issue daily doomsday warnings; you hear it just about everywhere you turn. When television actor David McCallum hosted a major prime-time series on ancient prophecies, he warned that every futurist from Nostradamus to Edgar Cayce to the architects of the pyramids to the Bible itself has targeted the year 2000 for the end of the world. All of this discussion, of course, has resulted in a publishing boom: Doomsday books and tabloids ring the chimes at cash registers across America in unprecedented numbers.

I've used several words to describe such date-setting . . . terms such as *unwise, harmful,* and *hurtful.* Yet somehow those words don't quite capture how I feel about such preoccupations.

Frankly, I think a better word is *senseless.*

Date-Setting Is Senseless

When you begin to set a date for our Lord's return, whose calendar will you use?

The current calendar in use in the West is reported to have been started by Dionysius Exegis in A.D. 532. His idea was to date year one from the time when, by his calculations, Jesus was born. Today scholars agree that Dionysius was off at least four years which means that since Christ was probably born in 4 B.C., the year 2000 actually falls in 1997.

But Dionysius was, of course, a late comer in the calendar game. The early Church was already operating by the Julian calendar which Julius Caesar had established because he was fed up with the errors of the Roman calendar. In the meantime, the Greeks had their calendar and so did the Egyptians and the Babylonians and the Anglo Saxons.

Is that what Stonehenge is? And the ancient Mayans and even the Muslims had to start with their own calendar.

Of course, the Hebrews were operating by a calendar dating retroactively from their calculated date for the creation, 3761 B.C. By that figuring, our year 2000 will be about 5761 on the Jewish calendar, not a very apocalyptic sounding year when you come to think about it.

Nowadays, of course, we have all kinds of technology and informed datings of the international fixed calendar and the world calendar and the perpetual calendar. And we could ask what calendar is in use across the galaxies, in the star clusters, in the nebulae. Is God going to have the last trump blown on the whole heavens in order to honor Dionysius' four year miscalculation back here on little, tiny Earth?

When the apostles crept up to Jesus at his ascension and put the question of the apocalyptic time to him, our Lord replied gently but firmly, "It is not for you to know the times or the dates the Father has set by his own authority, but you will receive power when the Holy Spirit has come upon you." Only God knows what time it is in Alpha Centauri, on the moons of Vega, in the Epsilon Andone system, or on Obi Island here on Earth. And only God knows when these times will run out. After all, the Bible tells us that God is timeless. He is the same yesterday, today and forever. So the next time somebody comes up to you and informs you that the world is ending in A.D. 2000, ask them, pull yourself up to your full height, look them right in the eyes and say, "Yeah? By whose calendar?" Be assured that God's clock is the only one worth setting your watch by.[6]

Do you see what I mean? Date-setting is senseless! Why would anyone do such a thing? Why would they try to calculate, in our calendar, a period of time that the Lord says we can't know anyway? It makes no sense. In fact, it is more than senseless; it is sinful.

Date-Setting Is Sin

In 1 Thessalonians 5 we read these words: "But concerning the times and the seasons, brethren, you have no need that I should write to you. For you yourselves know perfectly that the day of the Lord so comes as a thief in the night" (vv. 1–2).

Has a thief ever called you to schedule his burglary at your home? That would be a decent, polite thing to do, wouldn't it? Can't you just hear a call like that? "Um, if you've got your calendar handy there, I'd like to shoot for a week from Tuesday. Would it be convenient for you to be gone from your home? I mean, would that work out for you? How about 2:00 A.M.? Fine. Thanks for your cooperation."

When the Bible tells us that our Lord will come "as a thief in the night," it is making the point that *we don't know when that time is.*

It is unannounced.

It is unscheduled.

It is unexpected.

If any one thing is consistently taught in our Lord's Olivet Discourse in Matthew 24 and 25, it is this: Since we don't know the time of His coming, we need to be ready at all times.

Walk with me through these verses in Matthew 24 and 25.

- But of that day and hour no one knows, no, not even the angels of heaven, but My Father only. (24:36)
- Watch therefore, for you do not know what hour your Lord is coming. (24:42)
- Therefore you also be ready, for the Son of Man is coming at an hour when you do not expect Him. (24:44)
- The master of that servant will come on a day when he is not looking for him and at an hour that he is not aware of. (24:50)
- Watch therefore, for you know neither the day nor the hour in which the Son of Man is coming. (25:13)

And in Mark 13:32, a parallel passage, we read, "But of that day and hour no one knows, neither the angels in heaven, nor the Son, but only the Father."

All of these words were written concerning the Second Advent. But if those things are true of that event, they are just as true—and even more so—of the Rapture, which is the first part of the Second Coming. The Lord said you are not going to know the hour or day or week or year. Yes, it is imminent. It could happen at any time, even before the next beat of your heart. *But NO ONE knows when that moment will be.*

Before we leave this point, I'd like to nail down three truths in your heart.

1. No One Knows the Time of Christ's Return

It is pure folly to set a date for the return of the Lord. We don't know it. The angels don't know it. God the Father knows when it will occur and all we can do is prepare ourselves for that day—for it is coming soon.

I can appreciate the wisdom of the Father's decision to keep this matter hidden away in the counsels of God. If someone really did know in advance the date of the Lord's coming, he or she might decide to live in sin right up to the appointed week, then suddenly repent and get ready for the big moment.

"Come on," you say, "that's absurd! No one would do that." Oh yes, they would! I've been studying human nature through the thirty-plus years of my ministry, and that is precisely what would happen.

Other people would stop everything they were doing to sit on a hilltop to wait for His return. Remember William Miller, who divested himself of all that he owned, as did all of his followers? If we knew the day and hour of Christ's return, we wouldn't be able to make any future plans or establish long-term commitments or relationships. In His infinite wisdom, the Lord chose not to reveal to us the exact time of His return. He told His followers, "It's not for you to know. It's not your worry. You just go out there and be My witnesses—in your hometowns, in the neighboring towns, and then all over the world."

Personally, I'm thankful He set it up that way. I seem to have my hands full dealing with the past and the present. I'm willing to let the Lord handle the future. Perhaps you, too, grew up with the adage spoken so often in my home: "I don't know what the future holds, but I know who holds the future."

David wrote, "'You are my God.' My times are in Your hand" (Psalm 31:14–15). That's enough for me. When we try to bull our way into mysteries held in the heart of almighty God, we enter into domains where we do not belong. No one knows the date of our Lord's return. Don't let any man, woman—or angel—tell you otherwise!

Some folks have asked me why I get so upset with those who make specific predictions about the future. The simple fact is, there is only one rule for a prophet in the Bible. How do you know a prophet is a real prophet? Deuteronomy 18:21–22 tells us simply: "And if you say in your heart, 'How shall we know the word which the LORD has not spoken?'—when a prophet speaks in the name of the LORD, if the thing does not happen or come to pass, that is the thing which the LORD has not spoken; the prophet has spoken it presumptuously; you shall not be afraid of him."

If you read the rest of that passage, you discover that when a person made a prophecy in the name of the LORD and it did *not* come true, that man or woman was to be stoned to death. It was a capital offense without appeals!

I'm not suggesting we do that today, but one question keeps burning in my mind: If someone wrote a book and went on television or radio and said, "This or that is going to happen at such and such time; I guarantee it," and it didn't happen—why would you want to listen to that individual ever again? *Why?* I can't understand that.

Just imagine if I were to stand behind my pulpit at Shadow Mountain Community Church and say, "Friends, on January 1 in the year 2000, Jesus Christ is coming back. His feet will touch down in El Cajon, and we will all gather here on this campus to witness the event. Bring a sack lunch."

That might stir up a bit of excitement around here—until January 2. And then, I would be out of a job. I'd be making burritos at the local Taco Bell. Why should you ever come back to listen to me preach again? You shouldn't—and I wouldn't expect you to.

How could it be, then, that someone will go on record by setting a date for the Lord's return, and then—even though it doesn't happen—people go right on listening to him? People rush out to buy his next book. I can't comprehend it. It is wrong to make such predictions because the Bible says, "No man can know . . ."

For that matter, not even the angels know.

2. No Angel Knows the Time of Christ's Return

Not even the angels know when Jesus will return to the planet He departed two millennia ago. Look with me again at our Lord's words in Matthew 24:36: "But of that day and hour no one knows, no, not even the angels of heaven."

Think about that for a moment. The Bible says that no one in either the natural world or the supernatural world knows the day of Jesus Christ's return. The angels, of course, have constant access to the throne of God. They always wait before Him, listening for His commands. Isaiah 6 tells us they hover around His throne. Matthew 18 tells us they are in intimate communion with God. Jesus even revealed that angels will be the agents of judgment at the Second Coming and will gather the believers who survive the Tribulation. Yet in spite of all this, they don't know the date set by the Father.

My friend, we have been deceived and bamboozled. Can you imagine the brazen audacity of a man or a woman who would assert that he or she knows something that not even the angels by the throne of God know? What arrogance! And yet so many in the Christian community seem ready to lap it all up, again and again.

Strange as this may sound, I believe that many of these preoccupations have their source in Satan himself. Why? Because if we are standing around staring into the sky, we'll never get the gospel to Judea, Samaria, and the uttermost parts of the world. If we focus on mysteries we were never intended to unravel, we will neglect and abandon the Master's ongoing work in this day and time. We simply won't have time or energy to do the work of God. That, I believe is (and has always been) Satan's goal. *Those he cannot dissuade, he will distract.*

The angels don't know the date. And are you ready for a shocker? The Son of man didn't know either.

3. Not Even the Son of Man Knew the Time of Christ's Return

Do you believe that?

Look at Mark 13:32 again. Notice what it says: "But of that day and hour no one knows, neither the angels in heaven, *nor the Son,* but only the Father" (emphasis added).

Many people struggle with this passage. They wonder, *How can Jesus be omniscient and not know the time of His return?* But at the time Jesus spoke these words, He had voluntarily divested Himself of the independent use of His divine attributes. When Jesus uttered those words recorded in Mark 13, He did not know the time of the Second Coming. But when He rose from the dead and received His glorious resurrection body, He *knew.* And He knows now and looks forward to that glorious day.

That being the case, tell me—how in the world could someone discover what no *man* knows, what no *angel* knows, and what even *the incarnate Son of God* did not know when He was on this earth? Where does one go to get that sort of information? Christians need to believe what the Lord said about no human knowing the date or the time. If you are not willing to believe what Christ said about that, then why would you believe *anything* He said about His return?

There is only one who knew the time—our heavenly Father. And the very fact that we cannot know gives us reason every day for leading holy lives. We know that Christ is coming back, even though we do not know when it will be.

It is sinful to do what the Lord has told us not to do. The book of James tell us, "Therefore, to one who knows the right thing to do, and does not do it, to him it is sin" (James 4:17 NASB). To willingly, voluntarily deceive people by doing something God says you cannot and should not do is wrong. I would be guilty of the grossest kind of irresponsibility if I were to use my influence and do something like that as a pastor and preacher of the gospel. God keep me from ever seeking to persuade God's people regarding something I have no way of knowing!

But there is a subtlety to date-setting I want us to notice as well.

Date-Setting Is Subtle

Speculation requires nothing from you. Have you ever thought about that?

You may know how many toes there are on the beast in Daniel's vision. You may have memorized intricate charts on the book of Revelation. You may have twenty-seven theories on how to calculate the number of the Antichrist. But to know all that and not have the message come home to your heart is to be subtly sent down a cul-de-sac. It may even cause you—or others—to miss the highway to heaven.

Here are a few subtle things that begin to happen when you become preoccupied with prophetic times and dates.

1. Date-Setting Defeats Urgency

Titus 2:11–13 says this: "For the grace of God that brings salvation has appeared to all men, teaching us that, denying ungodliness and worldly lusts, we should live soberly, righteously, and godly in the present age, looking for the blessed hope and glorious appearing of our great God and Savior Jesus Christ."

That's the motivation for our life. If we knew He was coming back on the second Tuesday of next month, the only urgency we would have would be for a few days before then. But when we are not given the date, but rather given the assurance that there is a date, preparation will *always* be an issue!

While I was growing up, we weren't allowed to participate in a number of activities. One of the items on that list was attending movies. I remember preachers who would come to our church for evangelistic meetings and say things like this: "What if you were in the movie house *and the Lord came back?*"

Do you remember anyone frightening you with those words? *How would you like to go to heaven from the movie house?* That used to put the fear of God into me! I remember passing a movie theater as I walked downtown and feeling a little shudder travel up and down my spine. I remember thinking to myself, *I'm not going in there! No way, man. As soon as I walked through those doors the Lord would come back!*

One time when I was seventeen years of age, my parents went away on a trip and gave me the run of the house while they were gone. It was the first time they had ever done this. Home alone! They told me they thought I was mature enough to take care of things while they were gone, and that was that. Friends, I must confess to you, I let the dishes pile up . . . I let the laundry pile up . . . I let everything pile up. And the frustrating thing was that I didn't know exactly when they were coming back. I knew they would be coming home sometime within a three-day window—but I didn't know exactly when.

So you can guess when I cleaned up everything. It wasn't at the end of the three days; it was at the beginning. I had the house spick-and-span before that window of time arrived. Why? Because I wanted to be ready when my parents returned. I wanted them to be proud of me. I wanted to show them I was worthy of their trust. I didn't want to be ashamed when their car pulled into the driveway.

That's the whole purpose of teaching on the imminent return of Jesus Christ. We are to live in a constant state of readiness.

When you set dates—or allow others to set them for you—it takes away the urgency. That's the very reason why the Lord designed this program the way He did, so that we would always be ready.

I remember reading a story Dr. Charles Swindoll told in a book called *Rise and Shine* some years ago. Chuck talked about a time when he was in school, working in a machine shop. He worked with an old-timer named Tex. Ol' Tex had a kind of invisible sensor down inside. He seldom had to look at the clock. He always knew when it was getting close to that last whistle. Without fail, Tex was all washed up and ready to punch out a couple of minutes before the whistle blew. On one occasion, Swindoll reminded him that it was about time to start getting ready for quittin' time, and he never forgot that man's reply. He told Chuck, "I stay ready to keep from gettin' ready for quittin' time."[7]

I like that. How do you prepare for the Lord's return? You stay ready to keep from getting ready. Because if you do stay ready, you never have to scramble around to get ready, do you? And that's the impact the thought of the Lord's return ought to have on us. Because He may return at any time, we should live our lives as the book of Titus tells us—in a godly, righteous way, so that we might always be ready.

2. Date-Setting Promotes Apathy

When you lock in on a date for our Lord's return, you become mesmerized, which in turn causes you to lose your sense of direction. It also has a ripple effect on those around you. People may begin to respond to you as Peter predicted in 2 Peter 3:3–4. That passage says, in effect, "Since the beginning of time, people have been saying,

'Where is this so-called coming of the Lord? We keep hearing, *He's coming, He's coming,* but He still hasn't come. I don't think He's going to come at all!'" And they use that as an excuse for not preparing themselves or changing their lives.

The fact of His imminent coming should keep us always watching, always waiting, always urgently working. Every morning when we get out of bed and every evening when we turn out the lights, we should whisper to ourselves that this could be the day of all days, this could be the night of nights when we will see our Savior face-to-face.

In Romans 13 Paul writes: "And do this, understanding the present time. The hour has come for you to wake up from your slumber, because our salvation is nearer now than when we first believed. The night is nearly over; the day is almost here. So let us put aside the deeds of darkness and put on the armor of light" (vv. 11–12 NIV).

His coming is nearer now than when Paul penned those words. That's obvious, isn't it? For that matter, His coming is nearer now than when you received Him as your Savior. It is nearer today than it was yesterday. It is closer now than when you began reading this chapter.

With all my heart, I believe He could call us home *today.* I want to be ready for that moment, don't you? But you undercut that keen sense of urgency when you begin to set specific dates and times. You begin to live carelessly, rather than in perpetual readiness and anticipation.

Wendy Murray Zoba, associate editor of *Christianity Today* wrote about an occasion when her middle son, Benjamin, was very young. Benjamin had heard more than one sermon about receiving the Lord Jesus Christ. And the little guy certainly seemed well tuned to the heart of God. He was a kind, unselfish little boy and old enough to grasp the meaning of giving his heart to Christ. But when asked about it, he kept repeating that he just wasn't ready.

All of this troubled Benjamin's father. Why did his son resist talking about this crucial matter? And then came a morning when the family sat around the kitchen table eating their cereal and little Ben announced he was ready to give his life to Christ. He got up from the table and went upstairs. Benjamin's mom and dad looked at each other and decided they'd better follow. As they opened the door to his room, they expected to find their boy on his knees in prayer. Instead, they found him folding his Star Wars pajamas in his little Sesame Street suitcase.

"Benjamin," his dad said, "what are you doing?"

"I'm packing," he replied.

"Why are you packing?"

"Because I'm going to heaven."

And then that mother and father understood the reason why their child had hesitated to give his life to Christ. Benjamin thought that the moment he made that decision, he would have to leave his parents and literally move to heaven with the Lord.

The writer concluded that story by saying, it would be wonderful if we could all possess the faith of little Benjamin.[8] We should have our hearts so fixed on Christ's appearance that the attachments of our earthly life would pale in comparison.

When you think about it, every day we get up in the morning is our last day on earth . . . until God gives us another one. And just as little Benjamin left his soggy cereal to pack his suitcase for heaven, each day of our lives is filled with the promise and possibility of an immediate change in residence.

From the grind and routine of our workaday schedule . . . to a reunion in the clouds.

From the weights and worries of life on earth . . . to the wonder of our Father's house.

From the aches and pains of a deteriorating earthly tent . . . to a glorious new body that will be forever young.

From the frustrations and loneliness of life under the sun . . . to an eternal morning in the presence of the Son.

Because we know the Lord could come today or tomorrow, we

pack everything we can into the day God has given us. We should never allow our age or illness or hardship or work or anything else to take away from the excitement and the urgency and the adventure of living every day for almighty God. When you know that just around the corner everything will be resolved, you can live your life wide open for the Lord Jesus, always anticipating, always looking for His momentary return.

Benjamin had his pajamas and toothbrush packed. Whenever God was ready, he was ready.

Sons and daughters of God shouldn't live any other way.

Five

DO NOT BE BEGUILED

Beguile is a good Halloween word. It's another way of saying, "bewitched, bothered, and bewildered."

It's easy to fall under the spell of our prevailing culture. It's easy to find yourself in step with the crowd, marching along with everyone else to the same tune. It is so very easy to be shaped by, rather than shape, the attitudes that surround you. It's the difference between deliberately paddling a canoe against a river's current and allowing yourself to simply drift where that current will take you. The former requires exercise, diligence, and discipline. The latter requires nothing at all.

Our contemporary culture doesn't think much about the second coming of Jesus Christ. It isn't a subject for polite conversation in the right circles. It sounds too much like lunatic-fringe talk.

In days past this subject enjoyed a much higher profile. Before the advent of computerized type, for instance, newspaper composing rooms kept a wide variety of movable type in their production rooms.

And nearly every newspaper in this country had one giant-sized type to announce earthshaking events, such as the declaration of a war or the assassination of a president. In common parlance, this huge typeface was known as "Second Coming" type. Even in the secular world, the most momentous occasion anyone could think of was the return of Jesus Christ.

Today, just as technology has changed the way we make our newspapers, so our culture has changed the way we think about the second coming of our Lord.

The late A. W. Tozer wrote about what he called "the decline of apocalyptic expectation" in the contemporary church. Tozer felt that believers were forgetting the importance of Christ's approaching return and he compared that attitude to the generation just prior to his own.

> There was a feeling among gospel Christians that the end of the age was near, and many were breathless with anticipation of a new world order about to emerge.
>
> This new order was to be preceded by a silent return of Christ to earth, not to remain, but to raise the righteous dead to immortality, and to glorify the living saints in the twinkling of an eye. These He would catch away to the marriage supper of the Lamb while the earth meanwhile was plunged into its baptism of fire and blood in the Great Tribulation. This would be relatively brief, ending dramatically with the battle of Armageddon, and the triumphant return of Christ with His Bride to reign a thousand years.[1]

In recent years, however, the church has forgotten this truth. Christians, rather than being distinct from the world around them and living in expectation of their Lord's return, have become so much like the world that sometimes you can scarcely tell the difference between the two. Many churches reflect a careless, rather than serious, attitude toward the coming of the Lord.

This is not to say that we who are believers should be walking around with our heads down in some sort of doomsday mentality. That's not what the Bible is all about. The coming of Christ is not a negative subject; it is the brightest, most radiant star on the horizon. But it is also a teaching attended by stern biblical warnings. As God's people, we cannot allow those truths to be shunted off to one side.

In over thirty years of gospel ministry, I have watched evangelical preachers gradually change their attitudes about declaring the Second Coming. More and more, I'm hearing that the subject is "not relevant enough" to occupy a Sunday morning message. If you're going to talk about the return of Christ, it's being said, let it be in a seminary class-room—or in a weekday Bible study. But please don't spend an hour teaching "end-time" matters on Sunday mornings to people with family struggles, business failures, and a host of other emotional and physical problems. In the words of one pastor, "That is so totally irrelevant!"

Irrelevant?

I can promise you one thing with a strong degree of assurance: One minute after the Rapture, the subject won't be "irrelevant" at all. It will be the very definition of *relevant*.

A Dominant Theme

From whom, then, shall we take our cues about our Lord's return? From those who put the subject on a dusty back shelf, or from the Word of God itself? The Second Advent isn't a "back shelf" topic at all in the Bible. Both the Old and New Testaments are filled with promises concerning the return of Messiah to this earth.

I've done my homework on this! There are 1,845 references to that event in the Old Testament; a total of seventeen Old Testament books give it prominence. Of the 216 chapters in the New Testament, there are 318 references to the Second Coming, or one out of every thirty verses. Twenty-three of the twenty-seven New

Testament books refer to this great event. The four books that do not refer to it are single-chapter letters written to individual persons on a particular subject. The fourth is the book of Galatians, which does not specifically mention the coming of Christ, but certainly implies it. For every biblical prophecy on the first coming of Christ, there are *eight* concerning His second coming.

In light of such massive evidence, how am I to respond as a minister of the gospel of Jesus Christ? Do I just scratch off one out of every thirty verses in the New Testament and say, "Well, you know, that's not relevant"?

My friend, if the return of Jesus Christ to this earth is not relevant, then God the Holy Spirit would not have woven it through the eternal Scriptures. If He had not wanted us to ponder and consider these issues, He would not have underlined and highlighted them again and again. This isn't *my* emphasis; this isn't the pet subject or hobbyhorse of some mystic preacher. This is the word of almighty God, and He has so salted the Scripture with truth about the return of His Son that if I claim to be a teacher or preacher of the Word of God, I have no choice but to regularly visit this truth.

One of the positive aspects of being an expository preacher is that you have some built-in protection to keep you from getting off on special-interest areas or lingering on favorite topics. I grew up in an era when many evangelical pastors jumped from topic to topic, rather than preaching through a book of the Bible. And believe me, they all had their darling topics. You didn't have to sit under their preaching very long to know what those topics were. But if you teach the Word of God systematically and you are true to the text, you have to deal with *God's* priorities as they surface in the Scriptures from week to week.

And if you happen to be teaching through the Gospels, you will come to Matthew 24 and 25 and find yourself headlong in the second advent of our Lord.

Beginning at verse 36 in chapter 24, we read these words:

But of that day and hour no one knows, no, not even the angels of heaven, but My Father only. But as the days of Noah were, so also will the coming of the Son of Man be. For as in the days before the flood, they were eating and drinking, marrying and giving in marriage, until the day that Noah entered the ark, and did not know until the flood came and took them all away, so also will the coming of the Son of Man be. Then two men will be in the field: one will be taken and the other left. Two women will be grinding at the mill: one will be taken and the other left. Watch therefore, for you do not know what hour your Lord is coming. But know this, that if the master of the house had known what hour the thief would come, he would have watched and not allowed his house to be broken into. Therefore you also be ready, for the Son of Man is coming at an hour when you do not expect Him. (Matthew 24:36–44)

The disciples, you'll remember, had asked the Lord three specific questions regarding future events. His answer in the passage above came in response to the last question: "Lord, when will these things happen?" He had told them about the cataclysmic events that would occur at the end of the age. And the disciples were just as curious as we are. "When, Lord, *when?* When will all this take place?"

The Lord answered them but didn't give them everything they wanted to know. Instead, He gave them what they *needed* to know. Someone said that good preaching is giving people what they need disguised as what they want. Master preacher that He was, the Lord Jesus gave them just what they needed . . . and they were all ears.

The information contained in these two chapters of Matthew is primarily addressed to those who will be alive during the generation of the Tribulation. But believers today need to heed the voice of the Lord as well; He will come for us at the rapture of the church which will also be at an unknown day and hour.

So why should we concern ourselves? "After all," someone might reason, "if you can't know the when and the where, why even worry about it?" It reminds me of a question-and-answer sequence I heard some time ago:

Q: What's the difference between ignorance and apathy?
A: I don't know and I don't care.

That's the way a lot of people feel about the Rapture. They don't know and they don't really care.

Yet Scripture keeps repeating the theme of His coming over and over, like the clear tolling of a great bell on a frosty morning, *"Be prepared! Be ready! He's coming soon!"*

Some have tuned out the sound of that bell. They've grown used to it, in the way people become accustomed to the familiar chiming of a grandfather clock in the den.

Can you hear it as you turn the pages of your Bible?

Hear it in Paul's great rallying cry to the Romans:

And do this, understanding the present time. The hour has come for you to wake up from your slumber, because our salvation is nearer now than when we first believed. The night is nearly over; the day is almost here. So let us put aside the deeds of darkness and put on the armor of light. Let us behave decently, as in the daytime, not in orgies and drunkenness, not in sexual immorality and debauchery, not in dissension and jealousy. Rather, clothe yourselves with the Lord Jesus Christ, and do not think about how to gratify the desires of the sinful nature. (Romans 13:11–14 NIV)

Hear it in the apostle's strong commendation of the first-generation church in Corinth:

You come short in no gift, eagerly waiting for the revelation of our Lord Jesus Christ. (1 Corinthians 1:7)

Hear it again from his prison cell, when he penned timely encouragement to the Philippians:

For our citizenship is in heaven, from which we also eagerly wait for the Savior, the Lord Jesus Christ. (Philippians 3:20)

Hear it from the writer of the book of Hebrews, who urged his readers:

And let us consider how we may spur one another on toward love and good deeds. Let us not give up meeting together, as some are in the habit of doing, but let us encourage one another—and all the more as you see the Day approaching. (Hebrews 10:24–25 NIV)

Hear it from James as he wrote:

You too be patient; strengthen your hearts, for the coming of the Lord is at hand. (James 5:8 NASB)

Hear it from Peter:

The end of all things is near. Therefore be clear minded and self-controlled so that you can pray. (1 Peter 4:7 NIV)

Hear it from the elderly apostle John:

Little children, it is the last hour; and as you have heard that the Antichrist is coming, even now many antichrists have come, by which we know that it is the last hour. (1 John 2:18)

Hear the echo of that great bell in the concluding words of the Bible:

He who testifies to these things says, "Surely I am coming quickly." Amen. Even so, come, Lord Jesus! (Revelation 22:20)

What do you do with biblical emphases like these? Ignore them? Shelve them? Skip over them? Set them aside to deal with "more relevant personal matters"?

We practice such neglect, I believe, at our own spiritual peril.

If you go back through all those passages, you will find that in almost every one, the *future* truth impacts some *present* responsibility. It is the knowledge of His imminent return that puts urgency in our walks, determination in our service, and gravity in our decisions and conversations. "Work, for the night comes!"

Some Christians tell themselves they have a lot of time to win friends and family to Christ. We think in terms of "seasons" and "years," but we may not have seasons and years. We may not have the luxury of waiting for that ideal moment when everything falls into place and the door swings wide open. Why not? Because Jesus may come tomorrow morning! Jesus may come tonight at the stroke of midnight! And then it will be too late—forever, eternally too late:

"The harvest is past, the summer is ended, and we are not saved!" (Jeremiah 8:20).

Yes, it is common to hear people speak of "prophecy buffs" and smile indulgently at their preoccupations. And some do carry their interest to excess, even to the foolish degree of seeking to discover times and dates for our Lord's coming, as we discussed in the last chapter. Yet the truth is, the prophetic teaching of Scripture is some of the most practical truth in all the Word of God. We must not compartmentalize these great teachings into some obscure "curiosity corner" out of the mainstream of our daily lives. We must not shrug off prophetic issues, saying, "The scholars will deal with that stuff. I'm just going to worry about raising my children and taking care of daily life."

Don't do that, friend! Because "the blessed hope" of His coming will impact your daily life like nothing else! In the remaining pages of this chapter, I want to identify three attitudes that our Lord warned against in Matthew 24.

Jesus Warned Against a Cavalier Attitude

In Matthew 24:37–39, Jesus uses an illustration that would have sparked immediate recognition in every one of His listeners.

> But as the days of Noah were, so also will the coming of the Son of Man be. For as in the days before the flood, they were eating and drinking, marrying and giving in marriage, until the day that Noah entered the ark, and did not know until the flood came and took them all away, so also will the coming of the Son of Man be.

Jesus said that when the Son of man returns, it will be the way it was before the Flood. What was it like then? Genesis 6:5 tells us that when the Lord looked down upon His creation He "saw that the wickedness of man was great in the earth, and that every intent of the thoughts of his heart was only evil continually."

Now, today's culture may not be quite "there," but who can deny we're headed in that direction? Contrary to the fondest hopes of the evolutionist, this world is not growing better and better. In fact, it is precisely the opposite.

And the thoughts of men's minds? You wonder sometimes when you see the vile stuff reported in the newspaper pages or during the six o'clock news. How could anyone ever think up something so evil? That's the way it was just before the Flood.

But I want you to understand that the growing evil on this planet is *not* what the Lord was talking about when He spoke of the "eating and drinking" that went on before the Flood. I've heard preachers say, "You see how terrible it was? They were out gorging themselves with food and drinking themselves under the table. Gluttony! Drunkenness!"

Well then, what are you going to do with the rest of it? What about the phrase that says they were "marrying and giving in marriage"? That sounds almost wholesome.

No, Jesus is not speaking primarily of humanity's evil activities in this passage; His message is rather that people across the world in that day were all caught up in doing "ordinary" things. They were cooking meals. They were drawing water from their wells. They were celebrating weddings. They were taking life as it was, day by day.

And they were completely ignoring the warnings of Noah.

Life went on, and that fanatic from the religious right kept building a ship the size of a football field and talking about "rain"—whatever that was. So they didn't pay any attention.

How long did Noah preach to these people about the coming flood? Do you remember? *One hundred twenty years!* That's a long time to preach one message. How many different ways can you say, "It's gonna rain"? But that's the message he brought. Faithfully. Repeatedly. Passionately. That's what this "preacher of righteousness" did.

And everybody passed it off with a smile, a shrug of the shoulders, and a shaking of the head.

Noah's neighbors might have said of his preaching, "You're not relevant, Noah. If you must preach, talk to us about the real stuff of life. Talk to us about marriage and raising kids and earning a living. Don't keep harping on some future 'judgment' that nobody believes in anyway. Get a life, Preacher!"

Eating. Drinking. Marrying. Having kids. Working nine to five. Kicking back on the weekends. Life goes on. And rather than turning to God in repentance, the population didn't do anything; men and women drifted along with the prevailing culture, the prevalent attitudes. And the Bible tells us *that* is the way it will be before Jesus comes again.

It sounds a lot like our world today, doesn't it? Nobody has time for prophecy. Nobody wants to talk about the Second Coming. "Hey, I've got to go to a wedding this afternoon"; "We're having a dinner at our house tonight"; "We're going for a few drinks after work"; "We're having a baby in March"; "I'm takin' the grandkids to the zoo"; "I finally made manager; my career's finally startin' to hum."

So, just as in Noah's day, people move through life in a cavalier, heedless sort of way. They look forward to the future and take no heed of God's warnings. They live in the same way they have always lived.

The people of Noah's day ignored and even ridiculed his warnings. He preached for 120 years and not one individual outside his immediate family believed him.

He preached and preached and preached. He gave invitation after invitation. And then the last day of opportunity passed by, and someone, somewhere, felt the first raindrop that ever fell. Then the heavens opened up and the fountains of the great deep broke loose, and God closed the door to the ark.

Peter the Apostle has a word to say about this. Notice the startling parallels with today's world:

"First of all, you must understand that in the last days scoffers will come, scoffing and following their own evil desires."

And what will they say? Just listen!

"They will say, 'Where is this "coming" he promised? Ever since our fathers died, everything goes on as it has since the beginning of creation.'"

Doesn't that sound familiar?

"But they deliberately forget that long ago by God's word the heavens existed and the earth was formed out of water and by water. By these waters also the world of that time was deluged and destroyed" (2 Peter 3:3–6 NIV).

What is Peter saying? He's saying the time immediately before Christ's return will be just as it was during Noah's day. The public grew bored with Noah's preaching. Anyway, the old man was politically incorrect. He kept saying what people didn't want to hear. For as long as most people could remember, he'd been hammering away about "judgment" and an approaching "flood." But where was it? Where was the water? Where was the rain?

And because God's judgment didn't appear on their monthly calendars, these people assumed it couldn't be real.

Jesus warns against a cavalier attitude. You may have such an attitude yourself. You may say, "Oh, here we go again. Jeremiah's off on another prophecy trip. What's this? His second book on this stuff? Or his third? Doesn't he have anything else to say?"

I have written some books about this subject because it is important. And people who refuse to believe that's true will one day take notice of their surroundings with a different attitude. Members of their immediate family will be missing. They'll knock at the door of a friend's house and no one will answer. The car will be in the driveway and the lights will be on inside, but nobody will be home. And they will begin to wonder, as panic grips their throats, *Why didn't I listen when they were talking to me about the Lord's return?*

Jesus gave a second warning.

Jesus Warned Against a Careless Attitude

The Lord tells a little story in Matthew 24:42–44:

> Watch therefore, for you do not know what hour your Lord is coming. But know this, that if the master of the house had known what hour the thief would come, he would have watched and not allowed his house to be broken into. Therefore you also be ready, for the Son of Man is coming at an hour when you do not expect Him.

Jesus does not say that He is like a thief. But He uses the modus operandi of a thief as an illustration to make His point. In fact, the Bible uses that word picture a number of times.

Notice Luke 12:39: "Know this, that if the master of the house had known what hour the thief would come, he would have watched and not allowed his house to be broken into." And 1 Thessalonians 5:2: "For you yourselves know perfectly that the day of the Lord so comes as a thief in the night."

It's also in 2 Peter 3:10: "But the day of the Lord will come as a thief in the night, in which the heavens will pass away with a great noise, and the elements will melt with fervent heat; both the earth and the works that are in it will be burned up." Revelation 3:3 says: "Remember therefore how you have received and heard; hold fast and repent. Therefore if you will not watch, I will come upon you as a thief, and you will not know what hour I will come upon you." Revelation 16:15 adds: "Behold, I am coming as a thief. Blessed is he who watches, and keeps his garments, lest he walk naked and they see his shame."

What is Jesus saying? I believe the message is simply this: "Just because you don't see this taking place right under your nose, don't become careless in your attitude." Jesus warns against an approach that says, "I haven't been robbed this year, so I'm turning off my alarm. I'm leaving my doors unlocked. I'm not collecting the newspapers from the driveway. Nobody has ever robbed me. Nobody has ever robbed my neighbors. It won't happen to me."

Perhaps you could testify that real people do get robbed. Maybe you became careless or heedless, and the thing you thought would never happen, *did* happen.

That's what Jesus is saying. He is warning against a careless, reckless, self-deceptive attitude that keeps insisting, "It can't happen to me."

Yes, it can! Jesus Christ will return without any announcement. One day God will say, "That's enough," and His judgment will fall upon the earth and upon all who have rejected His Son.

But there is also a third warning.

Jesus Warned Against a Callous Attitude

Who then is a faithful and wise servant, whom his master made ruler over his household, to give them food in due season? Blessed is that servant whom his master, when he comes, will find so doing. Assuredly, I say to you that he will make him ruler over all his goods.

But if that evil servant says in his heart, "My master is delaying his coming," and begins to beat his fellow servants, and to eat and drink with the drunkards, the master of that servant will come on a day when he is not looking for him and at an hour that he is not aware of, and will cut him in two and appoint him his portion with the hypocrites. There shall be weeping and gnashing of teeth. (Matthew 24:45–51)

Jesus tells yet another story to make His point clear. He describes two slaves who work for an absentee master. One slave is good and faithful, the other evil and faithless. The first slave represents believers who will be on the earth before the Lord's return, while the evil slave represents the nonbelievers. The Lord declares that every person in the world holds his life, his possessions, and his abilities in trust from God, and every individual will be held accountable to the Lord for what he has done with that trust.

This evil servant displays the dominant attitude of callous procrastination. He doesn't really believe the master will come back anytime soon, so he has no motivation to cease doing all the evil things he has become accustomed to doing. Christ's word of warning to him is that he had better be careful because he doesn't know heaven's timetable.

Even as a pastor, I hear people say things like the following: "Yeah, I believe in the coming of the Lord. But I've got some wild oats to sow and some crazy things I want to do. I've got this all figured out. When I first begin to see anything that looks like the Second Coming, then I'll pull my life together and I'll be ready to go up."

First of all, I question the sincere faith of anybody who reasons like that. That's not the way a real Christian reasons. But even if you could reason like that, how stupid! What folly to do such a thing, for "in such an hour as ye think not," He comes!

Not long ago I was talking to a man about the Lord. He wanted to become a Christian, he told me, but it "wasn't convenient" for him at that time. So he put it off. I wouldn't want to be in that man's shoes if he continues to procrastinate and one day has to stand before the throne of judgment. Can you hear him mumbling as he stands before the Lord of the universe, saying, "Well, Lord, I was going to accept You and follow You, but—well, it just wasn't convenient."

Pretty lame, huh?

And the hard truth is, it won't be "convenient" for God to allow you into heaven . . . because it wasn't "convenient" for you to accept His provision for your sins.

William Barclay, one of the great historic commentators on the Scripture, relates a fable in which three of the devil's apprentices were coming to this earth to finish up their apprenticeships. They were talking to Satan, the chief of devils, about their plans to tempt and ruin man. The first devil said, "I know what I'll do. I'll tell them there is no God."

Satan said, "That won't delude anybody. They *know* there is a God."

The second one said, "I'll tell them there is no hell."

"You will deceive no one that way," Satan replied, "because men know deep down in their hearts that there is a place called hell and a punishment for sin."

The third said, "I know what I'll do. I'll tell them there is no hurry."

And Satan said, "You will ruin men by the thousands. The most dangerous of all delusions is that there is plenty of time."

In the mideighties I was working on a project about the book of Revelation, called *Before It's Too Late.* I came across a story about a time when the Pacific Northwest of the United States was witnessing a cataclysm unlike anything our nation had seen for generations.

Old Harry was a stubborn man. He had become a legend in the Pacific Northwest. Though he was warned repeatedly that his life was in jeopardy, he just laughed. Red flags and danger signs are often ignored, and Harry, well, he was just a picture of that kind of a person. He lived at the foot of a quiet mountain.

At least, she had been quiet for 123 years. Sometimes she stirred to spit cinder and ash or drool lava from her cavernous crater. Occasionally she looked down steep snow fields and rumbled a muted threat to the people who explored the lush forest and mountain meadows below. Some thought Bigfoot, the legendary giant beast, stalked her slopes. But Mount Saint Helens was seething inside, ready to unleash her force upon unbelieving admirers. She was awesome and mysterious, but only threatening to the few who understood her power.

March 1980, an earthquake measuring 4.1 on the Richter scale registered near Mount Saint Helens in southwestern Washington state. Forest rangers were advised of possible dangers from avalanches which could trap skiers or climbers. Most folks were unconcerned. The mountain setting was tranquil as people anticipated a time for renewal. The earth was singing with new warmth.

Then on March 27 a ranger heard what he thought was a sonic boom. The mountain had erupted. Scientists rushed to assess the explosive potential of the mountain. They painted a frightening scenario of future destruction. People listened, but many could not comprehend a disaster of such magnitude. Old Harry probably read the news stories while he ate a solitary breakfast and fed scraps to his sixteen cats. "Nobody knows more about this mountain than Harry, and it don't dare blow up on him," he bragged.

Days and weeks passed. Some became impatient with the geologists' negative reports. People would lose their concern of anything ever happening and wanted to get back to business as usual. Everybody heard the geologists say what they wanted to hear them say. They weren't really listening to them at all.[2]

When sheriffs' deputies ordered all residents on the shores of Spirit Lake at the base of the mountain to leave for safety, Harry said, "I'm having a hell of a time living my life alone. I'm king of all I survey. I've got plenty of whiskey. I've got food for fifteen years, and I'm sitting high on the hog."[3] Sunday morning, May 18, 1980, the mountain exploded and hurled pulverized rock and ash almost fourteen miles high. The force of the blast flattened trees, uprooting and smashing them like millions of dominoes spreading out from the crater. Steam, ash, and gases spouted from the incinerated vegetation. Mud floes flooded the rivers and transformed the beautiful mountain lands into a ghastly, charred landscape. The mountain's vengeance was five hundred times greater than the nuclear bomb that leveled Hiroshima.

The warnings were over. There was no longer any time to run. No one ever saw Harry again.

A scary story? Yes . . . and more. It is also a true picture of how people stubbornly refuse to listen to the truth, because their minds become filled with other things.

Don't be one of those people.

I don't want a single reader of this book to miss knowing Jesus Christ and spending eternity with almighty God. If you haven't trusted Him yet, why don't you do it today? Why don't you receive Him as your Savior and your Lord right now?

The mountain may not be erupting at just this moment . . . but can you feel the earth trembling?

Part Two

INSTRUCTIONS

Six

DO BUSINESS UNTIL I COME

One of the criticisms often leveled at those who believe in the Rapture and imminent return of Jesus Christ is that such beliefs lead to a life of laziness and indolence.

After all, we *know* He is coming back. We know the end of the story. We've read the last chapter in the book. Why should we entangle ourselves in the messy affairs of this passing world? Why should we soil our garments in the rough-and-tumble of the "culture wars" and the struggle for a more just and moral society? Why don't we just hold hands, sing songs, read psalms, and wait for the inevitable?

I've heard this caricature painted again and again—mainly by those who believe our primary task as believers is to "reclaim our lost dominion" over the earth. These folks insist that evangelicals who believe in Christ's forthcoming return have copped out on responsibilities for this world and its governance.

A few weeks ago, I happened to tune in a nationally syndicated Christian talk show. At first, I couldn't believe my ears. The host of this program just tore into evangelical believers—especially those who believe in the Rapture. His attack was so full of venom and sarcasm it was almost more than I could bear.

His line of reasoning went something like this: "You pretrib jokesters think you're just gonna be helicoptered outta here, so you're willing to sit back and let the world slide into wreck and ruin because you *think* you aren't going to be here anyway. You're content to sit on your hands and wait for the Rapture. What a surprise you're in for!"

The "surprise" to which he refers pertains to his belief that believers must endure the Tribulation—that Christ will not spare His redeemed bride from the judgment and wrath that will fall upon our world.

I have (at least) three problems with this argument. First, I resent the condescending tone. While this radio host may sincerely believe in what he says, his delivery system needs a little work. The bitterness and poison on his tongue do no credit to his position—or to his Lord.

Second, I think he has created a straw man for an opponent. I really don't know of anyone who subscribes to this "sit on your hands till the Rapture" stuff. I don't think I've ever met anyone who believes we ought to pull back from our involvements because of hope in His prompt coming.

Finally, our Lord Jesus certainly never left any such instructions. In fact, it's quite the opposite. I'm not a wagering man, but I would gladly take all the people I know who believe in the Rapture and put them up against any other group of believers in the world. Those who cling to "the blessed hope" have a deep sense of urgency about maximizing their life impact for Jesus Christ. Why? Because we realize the time may be short!

In a story told in the book of Luke, Jesus used a phrase that keeps ringing in my ears. In my heart, I believe it ought to be the watchword for all believers who long for His coming: *"Do business till I come."*

I love that. The old King James has "Occupy till I come," but for me, The New King James makes it more specific: "Do business till I come."

Here is how that line fit into His story:

"Therefore He said: 'A certain nobleman went into a far country to receive for himself a kingdom and to return. So he called ten of his servants, delivered to them ten minas, and said to them, "Do business till I come"'" (Luke 19:12–13).

A similar story is told in the book of Matthew. The latter parable dispels any notion of believers remaining idle while they wait for their Master's return. In this gripping story, Jesus gives us the key to our responsibilities as we wait for His coming:

"For the kingdom of heaven is like a man traveling to a far country, who called his own servants and delivered his goods to them. And to one he gave five talents, to another two, and to another one, to each according to his own ability; and immediately he went on a journey."

Do you notice the similarity to the first story? What Jesus describes must have been a fairly common situation.

Then he who had received the five talents went and traded with them, and made another five talents. And likewise he who had received two gained two more also. But he who had received one went and dug in the ground, and hid his lord's money. After a long time the lord of those servants came and settled accounts with them. So he who had received five talents came and brought five other talents, saying, "Lord, you delivered to me five talents; look, I have gained five more talents besides them." His lord said to him, "Well done, good and faithful servant; you were faithful over a few things, I will make you ruler over many things. Enter into the joy of your lord." He also who had received two talents came and said, "Lord, you delivered to me two talents; look, I have gained two more talents besides them." His lord said to him, "Well done, good and faithful servant; you have been faithful over a few things, I will make you ruler over many things. Enter into the joy of your lord." Then he who had received the one talent came and said, "Lord, I knew you to be a hard man, reaping where you have not sown, and gathering where you have not scattered seed. And I was afraid, and went and hid your talent in the ground. Look, there you have what is yours." But his lord answered and said to him, "You wicked and lazy servant, you knew that I reap where I have not sown, and gather where I have not scattered seed. Therefore you ought to have deposited my money with the bankers, and at my coming I would have received back my own with interest. Therefore take the talent from him, and give it to him who has ten talents. For to everyone who has, more will be given, and he will have abundance; but from him who does not have, even what he has will be taken away. And cast the unprofitable servant into the outer darkness. There will be weeping and gnashing of teeth." (Matthew 25:14–30)

Now, you have to admit, Jesus tells good stories. Can't you imagine His disciples getting caught up in that parable as He sat with them on the sunny slopes of the Mount of Olives? The story falls in the sequence of Matthew 25 in an interesting way. Just prior to telling this story, Jesus told the parable of the ten virgins—ten young women who were not alert and did not ready themselves for the bridegroom's return. As a result, these virgins were turned away from the wedding party and the door was closed in their faces.

This earlier story underlines the importance of waiting for the Lord and always watching for His return. But the parable of the talents, which follows, teaches us what to do *while* we are waiting. The bottom line? We need to be *working*. We're not to be sitting around drinking diet soda and playing Bible Monopoly. We're to be involved, energized, doing business for our Lord.

The parable of the talents warns us against laziness and passivity in our outward vocations. It warns us to keep our hearts with all diligence. While the first parable emphasizes attitude, the second emphasizes action. Both parables encourage us to watch for His appearing and to faithfully labor in the work of God while we wait for that great day.

The point of the "talents" story is to show us what we're to be about while we anticipate and look forward to our Lord's return. First of all, notice . . .

The Uncertain Return

A man traveling to a far country . . . called his own servants and delivered his goods to them. (Matthew 25:14)

In those days, long business journeys were inevitable. There were no airplanes, no trains, taxicabs, or rental cars. As a result, a business trip to another nation or distant city might mean weeks of travel. But what would the householder or business owner do about matters at home while he was gone? Commonly, he would give over responsibilities of his estate to trusted servants. Those servants were charged with handling affairs while the master pursued business elsewhere.

I can tell you this: If I lived in that era, I would be making fewer trips! Travel is complicated and disruptive enough dealing with high-speed transport. Not long ago I got on a plane in Cincinnati and the pilot told us, "We will be at the gate in San Diego at 10:24." He said that in Cincinnati. And when we rolled up to the gate in San Diego, it was exactly 10:24. I looked at my watch and thought to myself, *How do they do that?* But then we cooled our heels for ten minutes on the plane while the ground crew got the gates open. Go figure!

But modes of transportation were not so certain in New Testament days. When the lord of the household said, "I'm going to a far country," he had no idea when he would return—nor did his servants. Yet he expected those servants to be ready for his return every day. Every morning when those servants got up, the master expected them to be ready and available to give an account of their stewardship and their activities. What a powerful reminder that you and I are called to serve Jesus Christ in His absence, always looking for His return, even though we don't know when it will be!

Our Lord does expect us to watch for His return; yet as we watch, we are to keep working in His behalf.

Notice next that as he discharged the responsibility for the estate in his absence, he gave his servants some unequal responsibilities.

The Unequal Responsibilities

And to one he gave five talents, to another two, and to another one, to each according to his own ability; and immediately he went on a journey. (Matthew 25:15)

This interests me. Everywhere I go I hear people wondering why God did something for Jane or Joe that He didn't do for them. "It isn't fair," I'll hear them say. "Why do Jane or Joe have this privilege, or this opportunity, or this provision, when He hasn't done that for me?"

The hard truth is, we ought to be asking why God would ever do anything for any of us. As Jeremiah wrote, "Through the Lord's mercies we are not consumed, because His compassions fail not" (Lamentations 3:22). The only thing we "deserve" is His wrath. And if we have anything at all, if we are given any position of responsibility whatsoever, it is only because of God's great grace. Why in the world should we be measuring ourselves against anybody else's abilities?

I love Paul's gentle sarcasm when he wrote: "We do not dare to classify or compare ourselves with some who commend themselves. When they measure themselves by themselves and compare themselves with themselves, they are not wise" (2 Corinthians 10:12 NIV).

In the Matthew story, Jesus says, "And to one he gave five talents, to another two, and to another one." The "talents" spoken of here are not spiritual gifts or abilities, as the word implies in our culture today. A talent was simply a measure of money—a monetary term. (But we wouldn't be off the mark to apply the principle here to our gifts and abilities.)

So he gave one man five talents, another man two, and a third man just one. Please notice . . .

1. The Talents Were Dispensed According to the Judgment of the Lord

Why did the master in that story give differing amounts as he did? Jesus does not offer a reason. He simply did it because he was who he was. In the same way, God does what He does because He is Who He is. Who's going to question Him? Who's going to ask Him, "Why have You done this or that?"

Whenever God gives us an endowment or a responsibility, it is always according to His own judgment, His own determination. My friend, that thought ought to fill you with praise and adoration for almighty God for *whatever* you might have. Because whatever you've got, it's from His hand.

By the same token, however, you can improve upon what He gives you. I've told my sons that athletic abilities are God's gift; what you *do* with those abilities is your gift back to God. But the original gift is from Him, isn't it? That's what we read in 1 Corinthians 12:11: "All these are the work of one and the same Spirit, and he gives them to each one, just as he determines" (NIV).

Romans 12:6 speaks of our having "gifts differing according to the grace that is given to us."

"Who makes you differ from another?" asks the apostle in 1 Corinthians 4:7, "And what do you have that you did not receive? Now if you did receive it, why do you glory as if you had not received it?"

That's a good question, isn't it? If God gave it to you, why are you walking around all puffed up, thinking you somehow produced it for yourself? *God* gives us these gifts.

Here, then, is the story. The landowner goes away and gives to his servants different endowments. One gets five, one gets two, one gets one. Somebody says, "That doesn't seem fair." Don't be caught in that trap! Who are we to say that what God does or doesn't do is "fair"? God gives according to His own judgment, and His judgments are right.

Notice a second truth about that dispersal.

2. *The Talents Were Dispensed According to the Capacity of the Steward*

The Bible tells us the talents were given "to each according to his own ability." The fact is, God knows who we are and what we can handle. And so, according to that which He knows we are capable of by the power of the Holy Spirit, He fills the vessel that needs to be filled.

Do you remember the business concept that surfaced some years ago called "the Peter principle"? The original wording by the author, L. Peter, went like this: "In a hierarchy, every employee tends to rise to his level of incompetence."[1] In other words, people tend to get promoted beyond their capabilities. They start off knowing what they're doing and have a good handle on their tasks. By the time they're through being promoted, however, they're in way over their heads! God doesn't do that. He never promotes anybody beyond his or her capacity.

This gifting is not only dispensed according to the will of God and according to the capacity of the individual steward, but it is also given to us so that we might be complete.

3. *The Talents Were Dispensed in Order to Fully Equip Each Man*

The five-talent person wasn't any more "complete" than the two-talent man or the one-talent man. Whatever we have from God—if He gave it to us and He knows it to be perfect and appropriate for us—we are complete in that gifting. Just as the master left his servants in charge of various portions of his estate, so God has given every one of us what we need to accomplish His purpose for our lives. We all have what God wants us to have!

Now you've got the picture. The landowner went away and gave his three servants some specific things to administrate. He rode off down the road on his donkey and disappeared into the distance. Now . . . what must those servants do? They must discipline themselves to continue acting and doing business just as if the master were still with them.

It isn't easy to stay accountable when the boss isn't looking over your shoulder, is it? It isn't easy to keep the routine when you don't have to get up at such and such a time or punch a time clock. In this case, the boss couldn't check in by phone or fax or e-mail. The servants are simply left to do their work; he has to trust them to act in his best interest. And each of these employees responded. Two responded one way one responded in another way.

The Unusual Response

How, then, did each of the men respond to the trust placed in him by his master?

1. The Faithful Men Doubled Their Endowments

"Then he who had received the five talents went and traded with them, and made another five talents" (Matthew 25:16). Not bad! That's a 100 percent increase. That's "doing business," isn't it?

What about the next man?

"And likewise he who had received two gained two more also" (v. 17). He also doubled the master's money. That's good investment, good stewardship.

Which of them did better? Actually, they both did the same. They took what they had and increased it in the identical proportion. Which one had more? The one who had five—but he also had more to start with. Who had less? The one who had two—but he had less to start with. He took what he had, improved it, and made it something better than it was.

But what about the third man?

2. The Unfaithful Man Hoarded His Endowment

"But he who had received one went and dug in the ground, and hid his lord's money" (v. 18). This last employee didn't do anything with his endowment. He was so afraid of losing it, he probably took his shovel out to the corner of the estate in the dead of night and *buried* that solitary talent.

I can just see this old Fearful Charlie. Every morning when he was out walking the dog, he walked by that place where the money was buried—just to make sure it hadn't been disturbed. "Still safe and sound!" he told himself. "Boy oh boy, the boss is going to be so proud of me! I didn't spend one nickel of what he gave me. Put it all in the ground and covered it all up. When he gets back, I'm going to dig it up and hand it to him as he walks through the gate. He's going to be so happy."

But that man had the wrong approach. The faithful men doubled their endowments. The unfaithful man hoarded his endowment. Would his master truly be pleased? Everyone was about to find out.

The Unique Reward

His lord said to him, "Well done, good and faithful servant; you were faithful over a few things, I will make you ruler over many things. Enter into the joy of your lord." (Matthew 25:21)

I have taught this parable over and over again, and you can't get by these three things. There was a *commendation,* a *promotion,* and an *invitation.*

The two servants who had doubled their master's money were called before him. He commended them for doing business while he was away—for taking their initial investments and multiplying them. As a result, each received a significant promotion. "Well done, good and faithful servant. I have given you a little to manage. Now you are going to have much to manage."

Has the thought ever gripped you, my friend, that the way you pursue the Lord's business in this world today determines the kind of administration you will have in the coming kingdom? Do you ever ponder that? Perhaps in the Millennium, you will be the mayor of Chicago or Los Angeles. I don't know what your task will be. But I do know that the way you exercise your responsibility *now* will have a direct impact on what responsibility you will be given *then*.

To me, that thought is one of the greatest keys to stewardship in the Word of God. I've heard people say over and over again, "If you give to the Lord, He'll give back to you. You give with your little shovel, and He gives back with His big shovel. You can't outgive God." That is true. I believe that. Yet I think the principal reason people who give to the Lord end up receiving more is because God sees they are capable of managing what He has put into their hands! He takes note of their faithfulness, enlarges their capacity, and enlarges their responsibilities. That's how it works.

So, my friend, if you want to have more—in this life or the next—you had better manage what He has already given you as faithfully as you possibly can. The people God trusts with more are those who have proved faithful with little.

The Unthinkable Rebuke

You may find yourself identifying a bit with the fear expressed by the one-talent man. In Matthew 25:24 he said, "Lord, I knew you to be a hard man."

A hard man? I would say he proved to be a most generous and equitable man. But this third servant really didn't know his master. That was his first problem. That might be your problem too. If you don't know the Lord, if you don't know what kind of a Master He is, you will never trust Him.

The man goes on to say, "I knew you to be a hard man, reaping

where you have not sown, and gathering where you have not scattered seed. And I was afraid."

In other words, "I didn't trust you, lord." If you don't trust your
Lord, it's a simple fact that you will not invest your time and energy
and involvement in serving Him. This man failed because he did not
know and, therefore, did not trust his master.

> But his lord answered and said to him, "You wicked and lazy servant,
> you knew that I reap where I have not sown, and gather where I have
> not scattered seed. Therefore you ought to have deposited my money
> with the bankers, and at my coming I would have received back my
> own with interest. Therefore take the talent from him, and give it to
> him who has ten talents." (vv. 26–28)

The result of his failure? He was condemned. And why was he
condemned? He hadn't wasted his master's goods, like the unjust
steward in Luke 16. Nor had he spent all he had in riotous living, as
the young man in Luke 15. He was not ten thousand talents in debt,
like the unmerciful servant in Matthew 18. He hadn't done any of
those things. The point was not that he had done something wrong.
The point was that *he hadn't done anything*.

That's where so many of God's people find themselves in the kingdom today. It's not that they're doing bad things and undercutting
the work of God. It is just that they're not doing much of anything
at all. We talk about this all the time in our church family at Shadow
Mountain Community Church. We call it our "employment problem." Eighty percent of the people are cheering on 20 percent of the
exhausted workers. "All right! Go for it! Three cheers! Get it done!"

I believe if we allow the truth of this parable to really grip our
hearts, we would all be "fully employed," doing what we could until
our Lord and Master returns and calls us to account. This is not a time
to sit on our hands. This is a time for us to get busy for almighty God

as never before! This is a time for using every gift and ability He has so graciously given us to advance His Word and His will in our world.

"Well," you say, "that's easy for you. You're a preacher and an author. You know what you're supposed to be doing. But I *don't* know what I'm supposed to be doing."

My reply would be, "What has God put in your hand? What has He given you? What are your opportunities?" If you are a Christian, you (yes, you!) have a special gifting from God the Holy Spirit. Those gifts usually follow along lines you can identify in your own life. You may have the gift of helps. Or the gift of mercy. Or the gift of teaching and exhortation. Or the gift of administration. I know that God gave me the gift of teaching, and listen, *I do everything I can to multiply that gift, to manage that gift, and to use it with all of my heart.* If I don't do those things, I am an unfaithful, unprofitable servant, and the Lord will call me to account for that someday.

I really appreciate the J. B. Phillips paraphrase of Romans 12:6–8. Listen to this stirring list of imperatives!

> Through the grace of God we have different gifts. If our gift is preaching, let us preach to the limit of our vision. If it is serving others let us concentrate on our service; if it is teaching let us give all we have to our teaching; and if our gift be the stimulating of the faith of others let us set ourselves to it. Let the man who is called to give, give freely; let the man in authority work with enthusiasm; and let the man who feels sympathy for his fellows in distress help them cheerfully.

Whatever God has gifted you to do, my friend, do it! Manage that gift, make it work, grow it, develop it, practice it, and in God's wonderful grace, make it multiply. What God has given to you as an ability, give back to Him as an improved ability by managing it with all of your heart. That is what this parable is all about.

You say, "All right, Jeremiah, how am I supposed to be gainfully employed? Specifically, what am I supposed to do?" As I said, you pursue the areas in which God has uniquely equipped you to serve. But just in case you still don't know where to begin, I would like to add three more biblical imperatives that apply to every one of us, no matter what our gifting.

Three Places to Start

Wondering where to put your oar in the Lord's work? Let me give you three places to launch. If you are doing these three things in the power of the Spirit, you cannot—I repeat, *cannot*—go wrong. And I also firmly believe that as you plunge into the Lord's work, He will direct and guide you more specifically into unique areas of service for His name and His glory.

1. We Are to Be Busy Equipping Believers

And becoming equipped ourselves, in the process! When you know Jesus Christ may return at any moment, it changes the way you live. As one of my friends put it, "If you knew that at any moment the Lord Jesus were going to step through the clouds, right into your life, would it change anything?" Of course it would!

In his first letter, the elderly apostle John penned these words: "Beloved, now we are children of God; and it has not yet been revealed what we shall be, but we know that when He is revealed, we shall be like Him, for we shall see Him as He is. *And everyone who has this hope in Him purifies himself, just as He is pure*" (1 John 3:2–3, emphasis added).

The upcoming return of Jesus Christ ought to increase our godliness and righteousness before almighty God.

Notice the same truth in some selected verses from 2 Peter 3:

Therefore, since all these things will be dissolved, what manner of persons ought you to be in holy conduct and godliness, looking for and hastening the coming of the day of God, because of which the heavens will be dissolved, being on fire, and the elements will melt with fervent heat? . . . Therefore, beloved, looking forward to these things, be diligent to be found by Him in peace, without spot and blameless; and account that the longsuffering of our Lord is salvation—as also our beloved brother Paul, according to the wisdom given to him, has written to you. (vv. 11–12, 14–15)

Peter is saying that the Lord Jesus could come at any moment. And I am finding in my own heart that if I really believe that, if I really understand that, if I truly concentrate on that, it changes the way I live. In an earlier chapter we poked a little fun at the old attitudes of "not wanting to be caught in a movie house" when the Lord returns. But we don't want to make fun of that attitude to the point where we lose the emphasis of *living carefully* in light of His coming. It *does* matter what He finds us doing when He steps through the clouds. Someone has speculated that one of the reasons God will have to wipe tears from our eyes in His presence (Revelation 21:4) is because of our grief and shame over how He will find us when He comes.

Here is a second emphasis. Not only are we to be equipping believers . . .

2. We Are to Be Busy Evangelizing the Lost

In Acts chapter 1, the disciples were gathered around the risen Lord, just before He ascended into heaven before their eyes. What priorities did He leave with them at that final farewell?

Therefore, when they had come together, they asked Him, saying, "Lord, will You at this time restore the kingdom to Israel?" [Sound familiar? When, Lord, when?] And He said to them, "It is not for you to know times or seasons which the Father has put in His own authority. But you shall receive power when the Holy Spirit has come upon you; and you shall be witnesses to Me in Jerusalem, and in all Judea and Samaria, and to the end of the earth." Now when He had spoken these things, while they watched, He was taken up, and a cloud received Him out of their sight. (Acts 1:6–9)

Knowing the precise time of His coming is not important. But what is important is declaring His name and His salvation, near and far. Within your family and within your city. To your own neighborhood. To the whole world. Jesus says, "Don't be asking Me about times and seasons. Get busy and do the work."

Many of us have been caught up in speculations about computer bugs and about what the turning of the millennium might mean to our nation and world. And that's okay; I'm not opposed to the cautions and preparations. But in the process, let's not lose our Lord's strong emphasis. The precise timing of this event and that event are simply not important. What really counts is taking as many people to heaven with us as we possibly can.

Let me ask you a question. Do you have anyone in your immediate or extended family who has not yet come to know Christ as Savior? That ought to be one of the first things you put on your prayer list. Do you pray for that individual?

You say, "Well, Jeremiah, why wouldn't I?" I'll tell you why you might not. Because you and I get so busy, so involved, so preoccupied, so wrapped up and strung out by so many good and worthy activities that we put prayer on a low-priority shelf. Pretty soon weeks go by, months go by, and you suddenly realize you can't even remember the last time you prayed for your unsaved loved one.

There's a third priority.

3. We Are to Be Busy Encouraging the Church

You may possess the spiritual gift of encouragement, but if you don't, you should practice encouraging others anyway! Hebrews says this clearly in chapter 10: "And let us consider how we may spur one another on toward love and good deeds. Let us not give up meeting together, as some are in the habit of doing, but let us encourage one another—and all the more as you see the Day approaching" (vv. 24–25 NIV).

Earlier in that same book, the author exhorts us to "encourage one another daily, as long as it is called Today, so that none of you may be hardened by sin's deceitfulness" (Hebrews 3:13 NIV).

My friend, if you are convinced in your heart that Jesus Christ could return at any moment, you ought to be a champion encourager! Do it with words. Do it with phone calls. Do it with e-mails. Do it with hugs and words and prayer and flowers and gifts and smiles and heartfelt applause. Just do it! He is coming soon!

So what do we have on our plates as we anticipate His imminent return?

Building up fellow believers.

Reaching the lost.

Encouraging one another with all our hearts.

Does that give you enough "work" to start with? Will that keep you busy for a while? If any of you run out of something to do in those three categories, drop me a line at Turning Point Ministries, and I might have another idea or two!

Work While You Wait

Believing in the imminent return of Jesus is not simply a matter of "waiting," as important as that may be. It is rather a matter of *working*. Working hard. Working faithfully. Working in the power and joy and filling of the Holy Spirit. And when you work in such a way, you never know what God may be up to! You never know where your next kingdom assignment might be.

Someone asked me what I would like to be doing when the Lord comes back. That's easy. I would like to be standing behind my pulpit before my flock, declaring and explaining and applying the Word of God. For me, there's nothing better. There is no greater joy.

What would you like to be doing when He returns? Where would you like to be when the trumpet sounds, when the archangel shouts, and when in the twinkling of an eye we are changed and race into the clouds to meet Him?

What has He given you to do?

Do that.

Do business until He comes.

Seven

———— ❦ ————

EVANGELIZE UNTIL I COME

Last words ought to be listened to.

People often save their most important instructions, their most profound thoughts, their deepest concerns, and their most heartfelt expressions for last.

Pancho Villa, the infamous Mexican bandit, must have realized that as he lay dying. Bidding one of his compatriots to draw near, he whispered into the man's ear, "Tell them I said something!" And then he died. True story! The man had the right idea—he just didn't have anything to say.

Oscar Wilde, the celebrated Irish playwright whose wit and debauched lifestyle eventually brought him to ruin, was taking a last sip from a borrowed bottle of champagne. "I am dying as I've lived; beyond my means," he announced. Then, glancing around the room, the penniless and disgraced writer quipped, "This wallpaper is killing me; one of us has got to go."[1]

He went.

Many times, however, the last words a man or woman speaks before stepping into eternity can be extremely significant. Sometimes a dying individual may catch a glimpse of what lies ahead, either the glories of heaven or the terrors of hell.

Perhaps you can remember being a child and hearing your parents' last instructions as they stepped out the door, leaving you with grandparents or a baby-sitter. Your mom or dad knelt down, looked at you eyeball-to-eyeball, and spoke very plainly so you wouldn't miss a word. It was "Do this, remember to do that, be good, and we love you!"

The Holy Spirit did not miss the opportunity to record the last words of Jesus before He left this earth. And as we might expect, those words are deeply significant. In both the Gospel of Matthew and the book of Acts, we read our Lord's parting instructions to His disciples—and to all who follow Him—before He was taken up from sight.

Think of it! We have a written record of the very words the Son of God uttered before ascending to the right hand of His Father in heaven. And these are the words—perhaps more than any others—that Jesus wanted to echo in His disciples' ears as He left them.

He didn't say: "Organize a political action committee."

He didn't say: "Remember to work for justice and visualize world peace."

He didn't say: "Be tolerant of one another," "Save the whales," "Celebrate diversity," or "Commit random acts of kindness."

He didn't say: "Arm yourselves and take dominion over Rome."

What He *did* say was as clear as bright sunlight on a cloudless morning. There was nothing obscure or hazy about His final instructions.

Therefore, when they had come together, they asked Him, saying, "Lord, will You at this time restore the kingdom to Israel?" And He said to them, "It is not for you to know times or seasons which the

Father has put in His own authority. But you shall receive power when the Holy Spirit has come upon you; and you shall be witnesses to Me in Jerusalem, and in all Judea and Samaria, and to the end of the earth." (Acts 1:6–8)

These words echo the Great Commission given by Christ in Matthew 28:

Then the eleven disciples went away into Galilee, to the mountain which Jesus had appointed for them. And when they saw Him, they worshiped Him; but some doubted. And Jesus came and spoke to them, saying, "All authority has been given to Me in heaven and on earth. Go therefore and make disciples of all the nations, baptizing them in the name of the Father and of the Son and of the Holy Spirit, teaching them to observe all things that I have commanded you; and lo, I am with you always, even to the end of the age." (vv. 16–20)

What to Do?

Is it really all that difficult for you and me to figure out what the Lord wants us to do while we wait for His return? Is it rocket science? Is it truly so puzzling and confusing?

Actually, it couldn't be more simple. His words are certainly clear enough, regardless of the Bible translation we might choose. We either believe them or we don't; we either obey them or we don't. These last words of our Lord are to be the *first* concern of every believer. As you study the Bible, it's interesting to note that these words are not only His final emphasis; He emphasized them from the very dawn of His ministry.

In Matthew 4:19, speaking to those who would one day help found the church, He said, "Follow Me, and I will make you fishers of men." Throughout His ministry of three and a half years, He revealed His heart in this matter again and again.

In Luke 19:10, He told Zacchaeus and the crowds: "For the Son of Man has come to seek and to save that which was lost."

In Mark 10:45, when James and John came to Him to request places of prominence in the kingdom, Jesus used His own life as an example and told them that even the Son of man didn't come "to be served, but to serve, and to give His life a ransom for many."

As Jesus gave His great message on the bread of life in John 6, He declared that He had come down from heaven not to do His own will, but the will of the One who sent Him. And then He added: "And this is the will of him who sent me, that I shall lose none of all that he has given me, but raise them up at the last day" (John 6:39 NIV).

In our Lord's famous nighttime meeting with Nicodemus, Jesus told the bewildered Pharisee, "As Moses lifted up the serpent in the wilderness, even so must the Son of Man be lifted up, that whoever believes in Him should not perish but have eternal life" (John 3:14–15).

In John 10:10 our Lord said, "I am come that they might have life, and that they might have it more abundantly" (KJV).

Anyone who listens even casually to the words of the Lord Jesus quickly catches up with the passion of His heart. That is why, even as we study prophetic themes in Scripture, we must be very careful about allowing end-time concerns to distract us from the great passion of our Lord's heart. Remember what Jesus said to the disciples in Acts? "It is not for you to know times or seasons which the Father has put in His own authority" (1:7).

The book you hold in your hands witnesses to my strong interest in prophecy. I love to follow world news and keep my eyes wide open for signs of His coming. But, my friend, we can become so caught up in these issues that we walk right by people who do not know Jesus Christ. We can become so absorbed in these matters that we aren't even aware of non-Christians across the street from us—or even in the same room with us.

What would the Lord Jesus say about these millennial concerns if

He were to stand behind the pulpit in your church this Sunday? I think He would repeat what He said at both the beginning and the close of His ministry. I think He would repeat the last words He uttered before He returned to heaven. He would say something like this: "Men and women, learn all you can about the future. Watch for signs of My coming. *But don't forget, you are My witnesses.* I have told you to go into all the world and take the message of salvation to every man, woman, and child."

My friend, if evangelism becomes buried by eschatology, it is an unworthy grave. I found myself overwhelmed this past week as I went back to the New Testament and read again our Lord's final words. Just before departure He didn't say, "I'm coming back, and make sure you get all the prophetic nuances right so that you'll see it all correctly when I return. Go to work on those charts and over-heads."

No, He said, "I'm returning to My Father—and friends, you are My witnesses to the whole world. I'm counting on you to spread the word."

Our Lord made evident His deep concern for the lost not only by the way He spoke, but also by the way He lived.

The Life Jesus Lived

Encounters with people punctuated our Lord's earthly walk. Public and private. Men and women. Children and grandparents. Rich and poor. High and low. Esteemed and despised. Religious leaders and prostitutes. Soldiers and tax collectors. Priests and pagans. For three years Jesus wrote the book on personal evangelism. All of these encounters testified to His supreme desire to win and to save those who did not yet know Him.

When the time came for Jesus to select the men who would follow Him and carry on His ministry, He didn't give the candidates a temperament analysis or have them submit their résumés. When

Jesus selected those who would follow Him, the Scripture says He carefully chose men who would *do what He did*.

When He called His first disciples, He did not say, "Follow Me, and I will make you founders of the church." Nor did He say, "Follow Me, and I will make you experts in prophecy." From the very first day that each disciple began to follow Jesus Christ, he knew what he would be doing. He was called to be a fisher of men. He was called to be an evangelist to tell others about Messiah Jesus.

Andrew got the idea right away. Remember what he did? Scripture records that one of the first two men to follow Jesus "was Andrew, Simon Peter's brother. He first found his own brother Simon, and said to him, 'We have found the Messiah' (which is translated, the Christ). And he brought him to Jesus" (John 1:40–42).

In the words of Jesus, in the life of Jesus, and in the men He selected to follow Him, the Lord's continuing emphasis was on becoming fishers of men.

Time to Take Stock

These are crucial matters to consider as we contemplate the approach of end-time events. Depending on when you purchased this book, you are either about to celebrate, or have already celebrated, the dawn of a new millennium. Because of the confusion over which calendar to follow, few really know the precise date and time of that millennium's arrival. But it's a great time to take stock of our lives, isn't it? It is an anniversary—give or take a few days or years—of two thousand years since Christ walked on this earth. What should we be thinking about during this time? What thoughts should occupy our minds? How should we be responding to these momentous days as the sun sets on one century and millennium and dawns on the new?

Sometimes I think we just need to go back and reread the directions. We need to go back to the simplicity of what Jesus told us to do. Maybe we've strayed off course a bit. Maybe we've become a little too sophisticated for our own good. Maybe we've forgotten that the primary plan in the heart of Jesus when He instructed His disciples is *still* the primary plan. And if we don't go back and review that, if we don't let the Lord's words penetrate our hearts afresh, we might find ourselves chasing rabbit trails—and won't be any better for having experienced the millennial transition.

The disciples certainly got the idea after Jesus ascended. It took a little angelic nudge to get them jump-started, but after that they followed the Lord's specific instructions and returned to Jerusalem. They had been told to wait until they were clothed with power from on high. After Pentecost, after the Holy Spirit came upon them in power, they went out to follow the orders of their ascended Commander in Chief. In just a few short years they fulfilled the promise of Christ that they would do greater things than even He had done. Starting with a handful of men and women on the Day of Pentecost, that little ragtag band of disciples grew and multiplied until at the end of seven years, their number totaled at least a hundred thousand souls—and possibly many more than that.

No wonder the apostles were accused of "turning the world upside down"! The religious leaders of the day complained that these disciples had "filled Jerusalem" with Christ's doctrine. People were saying, "You can't go anywhere without running into this talk about Jesus."

So well did those early followers of Christ adhere to the divine purpose that, within three hundred years, the mighty Roman Empire was undercut and overthrown by the power of that gospel. By the middle of the second century, one of the great apologists said about the explosion of the Christian faith: We are everywhere; we are in your towns and in your cities; we are in your country; we are in your army and in your navy; we are in your palaces; we are in the senate; we are more numerous than anyone.

Why did that happen? Because everywhere these new believers went they shared the life of Jesus that had so transformed their own hearts.

The Church Jesus Founded

What did the early church have that today's church doesn't have?

We have so much more sophistication: big screens, television, radio networks, websites, tape ministries, beautiful facilities, trained workers, professional instruments, and on and on it goes. We have resources. We have tools. We have education. We have prosperity and comfort and safety. But do you know what that first-century church had? *It had one throbbing heartbeat of purpose.*

In his letter to the Romans, Paul wrote, "I thank my God through Jesus Christ for you all, that your faith is spoken of throughout the whole world" (Romans 1:8). In other words, "Everywhere you Roman believers go, people know who you are. The message of your faith in Christ has gone out ahead of you."

The apostle had a similar commendation for the believers at Thessalonica:

> You became imitators of us and of the Lord; in spite of severe suffering, you welcomed the message with the joy given by the Holy Spirit. And so you became a model to all the believers in Macedonia and Achaia. The Lord's message rang out from you not only in Macedonia and Achaia—your faith in God has become known everywhere. (1 Thessalonians 1:6–8 NIV)

Paul said, in effect, "We came here to Thessalonica to evangelize, but because of you, the message is already out there. Everybody's talking about it. We don't have to say a word. Everywhere you've gone, Jesus Christ has become the subject of conversation. You've made Him the issue."

Dr. Ferris Whitesell once wrote: "The New Testament churches were nerve centers of evangelism and in this respect constitute a pattern for local churches everywhere."[2]

How long has it been since you sat down and read the book of Acts straight through? What a fascinating account! You talk about a church on fire and growing! I went through the book of Acts recently and pulled out some of the phrases that describe the spread of the gospel in those days. Feel the strong, steady pulse of the young church in these descriptive phrases: "filled Jerusalem" (5:28); "went everywhere" (8:4); "in all the cities" (8:40); "all who dwelt at Lydda and Sharon" (9:35); "throughout all Joppa" (9:42); "throughout all the region" (13:49); "all who dwelt in Asia heard" (19:10); "throughout almost all Asia" (19:26).

You could call that saturation evangelism. It was like pouring water onto a thick sheet of paper and watching the moisture spread as the paper absorbs it—until it touches every corner. Jesus Christ was the subject wherever you went in that first-century world. His life, His words, His death and resurrection dominated conversations. People were coming to Christ by the thousands, being discipled, worshiping together, and winning still more and more.

Let's pick up a few more phrases from Acts—words that describe the church's surging numerical growth: "a hundred and twenty" (1:15); "three thousand" (2:41); "added to the church daily" (2:47); "five thousand" (4:4); "multitudes" (5:14); "a great many" (6:7); "many believed" (9:42); "a great number believed" (11:21); "a great multitude" (14:1); "a great multitude . . . not a few" (17:4); "many of them believed . . . not a few" (17:12); "many people" (19:26); "many myriads" (21:20).

What was going on during this period of seven years? It began with the Lord Jesus Christ and twelve guys—one who didn't pass the course. And because they believed their main purpose in life was not to raise money or build buildings or sell books or influence public policy or argue over prophecy, but to share Jesus Christ, their faith and joy sent shock waves throughout the world.

Anyone who knows me knows that I love prophecy. I study it, read it, ponder it, and am as interested in current events and contemporary prophetic signs as anyone. But I can't escape this one fact: If we know everything there is to know about prophecy and yet haven't got time to walk across the street and invite our neighbor to church or introduce him or her to the Lord, we are not following our Lord's last instructions.

Remember what Paul said? "Though I have the gift of prophecy, and understand all mysteries and all knowledge . . . but have not love, I am nothing" (1 Corinthians 13:2).

The last command of our Lord was His first concern: to go into all the world and declare His salvation, purchased on the cross.

The year 2000 is not only a time for us to look forward, but might also be a time to look back. How have we been doing? We have seen great missionary endeavors during our day. Most of us have lived during the greatest outreach of missions in world history. But the truth is, we're not keeping up. There are still many hundreds of millions of people who have never heard, not even once, the news that Jesus Christ died for their sins. And even in your own city or town, there are men and women and children who may know about "church," but really don't know a thing about Jesus or what it means to receive Him as Savior.

Why have we let this urgent imperative from our Lord drop from a number one priority in our lives? Why don't we follow His final imperative? There are a few reasons I would like us to consider.

The Problem of Proxy-ism

I'm not even sure there is such a word as *proxy-ism*, but we'll see if I can slip it past my editors.

You know what a proxy is. A proxy is someone who goes in your place. Back in the days of the Civil War, a wealthy man who was drafted into the army could hire a proxy to go to war for him and take his place in the terrible battles that claimed so many. Perhaps you have had to cast a "proxy vote" in some recent election. A proxy is simply a replacement.

In the church of Jesus Christ, we have developed proxy-ism into a fine art. It goes like this: "If you cannot go, you must send someone in your place." Many who know very well that evangelism is a command from Christ fend off their consciences by putting a check in the offering plate. Please don't stop doing that, friend . . . but *supporting a proxy evangelist is not the same as being one yourself.*

Some years ago, someone gave me this definition of a great missionary church. A missionary church is not a missionary church because it has a large missions budget, or because it sends many of its people to the field, or because it hosts an annual missions conference, or because it has a full-time missions pastor. A missionary church qualifies as a great missionary church only when it becomes a church full of those *who are missionaries wherever they are and wherever they go.* That's what the Lord had in mind. Institutional missions were never invented to take over the role of individual missions in our lives—and that is one reason why we are not reaching the masses today.

I don't think God wants everybody to go to Africa or India. Maybe not even to Haiti or Mexico or Utah. But God wants everybody to go somewhere—to their business places, to their neighbors, to their children, to their communities. He has commanded all of us to have a heart and a passion for evangelism. We may not win many, but we are always to be on the alert for opportunities to declare our faith.

We are living in an era of ultrasensitive "tolerance" for every lifestyle under the sun. Our nation's underlying philosophy of "moral relativism" dictates that one set of beliefs is every bit as valid as another. What you believe is "truth for you," and what I believe is "truth for me," and woe to me if I question the validity of your "truth"!

That's a philosophy that takes people to hell every day.

Only one truth saves. Only one gospel brings eternal life. There is only one escape from hell. We need to go to men and women and children with the precious gospel of Jesus Christ and declare His love for them. The same gospel that worked in your parents' generation will work today because, as Paul put it, "it is the power of God unto salvation." It is eternally relevant. It still changes lives.

Sometimes we do not follow the Lord's command because of proxy-ism. What are other reasons why we don't obey His command?

The Problem of Professionalism

I've heard this again and again during my years of pastoral ministry: "Pastor, what do you mean you want us to tell people about the Lord? That's what we pay you to do. That's your job. I never went to seminary. I was never called into the ministry. What's the problem? Do you need a little more money to get the job done? Fine, we'll give you more money, and you be a witness for Him."

But that's not what the Word of God says, is it? My job isn't to do the work of the ministry (though I am a sheep also and have the same responsibility to witness as anyone else). My job as pastor-teacher is to equip the people of God to perform the work of evangelism. (See Ephesians 4:11–12.) If your pastor is the only evangelist in your church, your outreach will be extremely limited. But if all the members of the body are equipped and motivated to declare the salvation of Christ, the ministry is multiplied—many, many times.

You say, "How do I do it?"

There are numerous clear, simple methods you can learn and use if you really desire to do it. Outstanding little booklets such as *The Four Spiritual Laws* or *The Bridge* or *Steps to Peace with God* can be a great help in explaining the gospel. Carry those little booklets with you wherever you go . . . in your pocket . . . in your purse . . . in your car . . . in your Day-Timer. These will help you present the message of salvation in a simple, sequential way. Leave these booklets with people in a gracious way. (By the way, don't leave them on a restaurant table in place of a tip! Waitresses tell me Christians do that all the time, and it is neither effective nor appreciated! If you plan on leaving a piece of literature, wrap that booklet in green and it just might get read.)

There is yet another way we seek to dodge our Lord's command.

The Problem of Protective-ism

When our church dropped its "Baptist" label and become "Shadow Mountain Community Church," people worried that non-Baptists might start coming. And I said, "Wonderful!" As a matter of fact, no one knows who was what denomination anymore. It doesn't matter! *Everyone* is a candidate for heaven if they will put their trust in Jesus Christ.

Someone told me a long time ago that when we get to heaven our tags aren't going to matter because God will take them off. If you go to hell, they'll burn off! So quit worrying about labels.

The Problem of Pessimism

"What good will it do?" I hear people say. "They won't believe. People just get offended." We hear a lot of criticism these days about evangelical Christians being "too aggressive." As I mentioned earlier, it isn't culturally correct to evangelize today. You're supposed to be tolerant. You're supposed to value "sincerity" above all else. If everybody is sincere about what they believe, that's all that matters.

Have you ever been totally lost when you were sincerely trying to find an address? I found myself in that situation just last week. It was so frustrating! I was trying to find an airport and felt sure I was traveling in the right direction. But as it turned out, I was going exactly the opposite direction from the airport. *Sincerity is worthless if it is not based upon truth.* Solomon wrote, "There is a way which seems right to a man, but its end is the way of death" (Proverbs 14:12). And Jesus didn't say, "I am one of the ways." Jesus said, "I am *the* way, *the* truth, and *the* life. No man comes to the Father except through Me" (John 14:6, emphasis added).

Friend, we have to start believing that again. There is only one way into heaven, and that's through Jesus Christ. Without Him, people are *lost* and have no hope. "Well," you say, "you have to water down the message a little because we live in a multicultural society." No, we don't! We live in a society filled with people who need the Lord Jesus Christ. Cut through all that cultural, relativistic garbage and get them to the Savior. I believe with all my heart that is what the Lord is saying to His church at the turning of the millennium.

Suppose we knew somehow that we had only one year left. (I'm not saying it is one year. I'm using this as an illustration.) Suppose you learned for sure that there was only one year remaining before the Lord Jesus called His church home, setting the stage for the Great Tribulation on earth. What would the Lord have us do in such a case? Stockpile food? Earn a lot of money? Pursue a political agenda? No, I think He would say, "Friends, you've got one year left to go up and down the highways and byways and corridors of this land with the good news of My salvation and provision for sin. Share that message as never before! Sell everything you have to buy literature and get it to those who don't know. Give everything you own so that by the time I come back at the end of this year, you will have touched every human being you could possibly touch with the message of Jesus Christ, the Lord of Glory."

Years ago when I first started out in the ministry, I got a little magazine called the *Pulpit Digest*. I hardly ever read it, but once in a while I came across a story in that publication that made it almost worth the subscription. Like this gem:

Whatever Became of Evangelism?
Now it came to pass that a group existed who called themselves fishermen. And lo, there were many fish in the waters all around. In fact,

the whole area was surrounded by streams and lakes filled with fish. And the fish were hungry.

Week after week, month after month, and year after year, those who called themselves fishermen met in meetings and talked about their call to fish, the abundance of fish, and how they might go about fishing. Year after year they carefully defined what fishing means, defended fishing as an occupation, and declared that fishing is always to be a primary task of fishermen.

These fishermen built large, beautiful buildings for local fishing headquarters. The plea was that everyone should be a fisherman and every fisherman should fish. One thing they didn't do, however; they didn't fish.

In addition to meeting regularly, they organized a board to send out fishermen to other places where there were many fish. The board was formed by those who had the great vision and courage to speak about fishing, to define fishing, to promote the idea of fishing in faraway streams and lakes where many other fish of different colors lived. Also the board hired staffs and appointed committees and held many meetings to define fishing, to defend fishing, to decide what new streams should be thought about. But the staff and committee members did not fish.

Large, elaborate, and expensive training centers were built whose original and primary purpose was to teach fishermen how to fish. Over the years, courses were offered on the needs of the fish, the nature of fish, how to define fish, the psychological reactions of fish, and how to approach and feed fish. Those who taught had doctorates in "fishology." But the teachers did not fish. They only taught fishing.

Further, the fishermen built large printing houses to publish fishing guides. Presses were kept busy night and day to produce materials solely devoted to fishing methods, equipment, and programs, to arrange and encourage meetings, to talk about fishing. A speaker's bureau was also provided to schedule special speakers on the subject of fishing.

After one stirring meeting on "The Necessity of Fishing," one young fellow left the meeting and went fishing. The next day he reported that he had caught two outstanding fish. He was honored for his excellent catch and scheduled to visit all the big meetings possible to tell how he did it. So he quit his fishing in order to have time to tell about the experience to the other fishermen. He was also placed on the Fishermen's General Board as a person having considerable experience.

Imagine how hurt some were when one day a person suggested that those who don't fish were not really fishermen, no matter how much they claimed to be. Yet it did sound correct. Is a person a fisherman if year after year he never catches a fish? After all, were they not following the Master who said, "Follow Me, and I will make you fishers of men" (Matthew 4:19)? Is one following if he isn't fishing?[3]

I don't write books or preach sermons to make people feel guilty. That is not my purpose. Every one of us—myself included—could be doing a better job of telling other people about our Lord. Sometimes I get on an airplane to come home from some speaking assignment in another part of the country, and I'm seated by someone who most likely doesn't know the Lord. I may be weary on that flight. I may have a dozen things to do or write down before I get home. Yet here is a person I will never be with again for the rest of my life—and he or she is strapped into a seat next to me.

Then sometimes the Lord sends along a little turbulence on that flight—and that individual sitting next to me takes more and more interest in the Bible I have open on my tray. It is so very, very easy to let those opportunities just slip by, isn't it? Paul's words to the Ephesians take us all to task: "Be very careful, then, how you live—not as unwise but as wise, making the most of every opportunity, because the days are evil" (Ephesians 5:15–16 NIV).

Now, I'm not talking about buttonholing people or being obnoxious. That's not what we are to do. I'm just talking about beginning each day by praying, "Lord, today I want to live for You. And Lord, if You bring someone across my path today who needs You, help me to sense it. And help me to do the right thing."

Andrew went to find his brother Peter and said, "I have Someone I can't wait for you to meet. Come with me." And he brought his brother to Jesus.

It was just that simple.

It still is.

Eight

EDIFY ONE ANOTHER
UNTIL I COME

The demolition ball has been swinging in America this year, and walls have been falling all around us.

It has been a year of scandal, denials, recriminations, brazen defiance, and national shame. It has been a year when people at the very pinnacle of national leadership have seemed determined to tear down everything important to our country's future.

We have torn down integrity . . . truth . . . purity . . . honesty . . . and respect. We have demolished the very things many of us have longed to rebuild in our nation. Not since the Vietnam War has our population been so divided and embittered. From talk radio to letters to the newspaper to the very halls of Congress, Americans seem intent on putting their own spin on these shameful events.

And we've been tearing one another down in the process.

Frankly, it sounds very much like the culture Paul prophesied would be in place just before the return of the Lord. Eugene Peterson's *Message* paraphrase puts it like this:

Don't be naive. There are difficult times ahead. As the end approaches, people are going to be self-absorbed, money-hungry, self-promoting, stuck-up, profane, contemptuous of parents, crude, coarse, dog-eat-dog, unbending, slanderers, impulsively wild, savage, cynical, treacherous, ruthless, bloated windbags, addicted to lust, and allergic to God. They'll make a show of religion, but behind the scenes they're animals. Stay clear of these people. (2 Timothy 3:1–4)

The destruction and demolition don't stop at the Potomac River. They have a ripple effect reaching across our nation, dividing communities and undermining so many of the values we cherish.

But I want to write about something better—an alternative to this wholesale demolition. Because, you see, while we cannot stop the erosion and the tearing down of biblical values in our culture before our Lord's return—we *can* do something about building one another up.

In fact, we must.

"Feed My Sheep"

The final chapter of John's Gospel records one of the last conversations between the resurrected Lord Jesus and Peter.

You may remember that brief, poignant exchange. The disciples had been fishing, and as they headed for shore, they were met by the risen Christ. He called them to a fragrant breakfast, prepared over hot coals. Just days earlier, Peter had denied his Lord beside a fire. Now, beside another fire, he will be restored. Just as Peter had denied Christ three times in his earlier experience, he would be given three opportunities to confess his love for Jesus.

That's the portion of the story most people remember. Jesus uses one word for love—a strong, intense word for committed love—and Peter, his confidence shattered, comes back with a weaker word in reply. That happens three times, until finally Jesus looks Peter in the eyes and uses Peter's own, weaker word, as if to say, "Peter, do you even care for Me as a friend?"

The question breaks the big fisherman's heart, but Jesus neither rejects nor casts the sorrowing man aside. On the contrary, He recommissions Peter for service in the kingdom. In no uncertain terms, He gives him a job to do.

That is the portion of the story so often overlooked. Every time Peter answered the Lord, the Lord gave him a strong, specific command: "Feed My lambs, Peter"; "Tend My sheep, Peter"; "Feed My sheep, Peter."

Did Peter get the message? He really did, didn't he? Years later, he would take pen in hand and write:

> Shepherd the flock of God which is among you, serving as overseers, not by constraint but willingly, not for dishonest gain but eagerly; nor as being lords over those entrusted to you, but being examples to the flock; and when the Chief Shepherd appears, you will receive the crown of glory that does not fade away. (1 Peter 5:2–4)

I wonder sometimes what the Chief Shepherd would say to His church today if AT&T could establish a direct phone link between earth and heaven. Can't you just imagine it? On a given Sunday morning, Jesus speaks simultaneously via satellite to congregations all over the world. You're sitting there in your pew, your heart beating fast. What will He say? What will His instructions be as the church age draws to a close?

Head for the Ozarks with a year's supply of food?

Throw up your arms in despair?

Run for office?

Go out on the soapbox circuit and rant and rail against the culture and its problems?

No, I have a hunch His message would be the same one He gave before He ascended into heaven from that spot outside Jerusalem.

"You shall be witnesses to Me . . . to the end of the earth." And after He said that, I think He would certainly repeat the words He spoke three times to Peter: *"Feed My sheep."*

In other words, "Brothers and sisters in the church, you live in a time of terrible demolition. My eyes miss nothing. I have seen it all. But even while precious things all around you are being torn down and dismantled, you can be in the midst of building. Build up My church! Take care of My sheep. Feed them. Tend them. Love them . . . as I have loved you."

Building Up His People

We don't need a direct phone line, do we? We don't need a satellite connection to heaven. He has given us His inerrant Word, which is a light to our feet and a lamp to our path. He has given us His Holy Spirit to dwell within us, illuminating the pages of Scripture, reminding us of everything Jesus taught.

And leaping out of those pages is a word that speaks to our mission as believers in a clear and specific way. It's the word *edification.*

You may have heard that term tossed around if you've spent much time in evangelical circles. It's one of those "spiritual"-sounding terms we sometimes hear in church. It certainly sounds impressive, but *what does it really mean?*

Actually, it's pretty simple. The Greek term is made up of two words: One means "house" and the other, "to build." To edify, then, means to "build the house."

That's it. That's all. Build the house.

Jesus used the term literally in Matthew 7:24 when He said, "Therefore whoever hears these sayings of Mine, and does them, I will liken him to a wise man who *built his house* on the rock" (emphasis added).

Again, in Luke 6:48, Jesus speaks about "a man *building a house,* who dug deep and laid the foundation" (emphasis added). Back in

Matthew 24:1, the Bible uses the term to speak of the buildings of the temple.

I will never forget the process of building the worship center for our church here in El Cajon. It was exciting for us, a vision taking shape before our eyes. Even now I can visualize every step of the process: from the time the first backhoe dug the first scoop of dirt on that empty lot until they laid the brand-new carpet in the finished building.

We get excited about building buildings and seeing them take shape. The New Testament, however, is much more concerned about building people. Most often in Scripture, *edify* is used in a metaphorical sense to mean "build up one another." Build up the body of Christ. Build up fellow believers. That, I believe, is what you and I are to be about as the last days come upon us.

It's a sad story, but I have met scores of people here at our church who say, "Please don't ask me to do anything. Don't ask me to say anything. Just let me come and heal for a while. You can't believe how I was torn down at our last church. I need time to be built back up."

When a church doesn't function according to the pattern of the Word of God, it can be one of the most destructive places anywhere. How that must grieve the heart of the Master Builder!

With all my heart, I want this year of my life to be a *building* year. I'm not speaking of physical buildings, though some may be built. I'm referring to the building of God's people. That's the passion of my heart. That's why I get up every morning. I want to build up— or *edify*—the body of Christ until He comes or calls me home.

One of the most important statements from the lips of our Savior is these words of Matthew 16:18. He said, "I will build My church, and the gates of Hades shall not prevail against it." Was Jesus talking about some brick and stone structure with a steeple on top? No, He was talking about the worldwide body of believers.

The church is built up *externally* through evangelism. We add people to the body as we baptize them and they become part of the church. But the church is built up *internally* through edification, through how we strengthen, encourage, and minister to one another in the body of Christ. And my friend, I am convinced that if ever there was a time when we needed to concentrate on building up one another, it is during this era of history—when values and morality and everything we hold dear seem up for grabs.

Let's face it, when you walk out into the world, you walk into an environment that automatically tears you down. Christians are no longer viewed with favor by our culture. Our beliefs and concerns are under attack in the schools, in the universities, in the entertainment industry, and in the mainstream media. It's hostile out there. We can get beaten up just going about our business.

We gather with our brothers and sisters to get built back up, so we can go back into the world and face the challenges again. That process has to be an intentional goal of every one of us, or we will be victimized by our culture.

In another word picture, Scripture refers to believers as "living stones" in a building being constructed by the Lord. Peter writes: "You also, as living stones [that's you and me], are being built up a spiritual house, a holy priesthood, to offer up spiritual sacrifices acceptable to God through Jesus Christ" (1 Peter 2:5).

We are the building, a living entity that spans culture and language, heaven and earth, time and eternity. Our church building in southern California is a beautiful place and we love it. But do you know what? The Church isn't *in* this building when all the people leave. The Church isn't in your worship center when the people have departed. When you leave, the Church leaves.

The real Church is not the building: It is people. Redeemed men and women. If you moved your whole congregation out to the parking lot one Sunday, the Church wouldn't be in the building anymore. The Church would be out in the open air. Paul said as much to the Corinthians:

"For we are God's fellow workers; you are God's field, you are God's building" (1 Corinthians 3:9).

Do you see that? We are the building of God! We build it up externally through evangelism when we add people to it. But we build it up internally by strengthening and encouraging and ministering to the members of the body so that they have the strength to serve God in a world that is hostile to everything we believe.

What Is Edification All About?

When you survey the word *edification* through Scripture, it's amazing the things you can learn.

It's Not About Yourself; It's About the Saints

You and I are called to build up and strengthen one another. I am called to build you up. You are called to build me up. I must be very careful not to tear you down by my actions, inaction, or words.

I heard about a young preacher who began one of his messages by asking his congregation for honest feedback. "I want to get better at this," he told them. "And when I get done, I hope you'll tell me how I'm doing."

Now, it's a risky thing to open yourself up like that, because there are those (for whatever reason) who take perverse delight in being hypercritical. Such was the case with an older gentleman who approached the young man afterward. "The first thing I need to tell you," he said, "is you *stunk.*"

"Oh, my word!" said the pastor. "That's terrible! Can you be more specific? Can you help me a little here?"

The old man was more than happy to comply. "I'll give you three things," he sniffed. "Number one: You read your sermon. Number two: You read it poorly. And number three: It wasn't worth reading in the first place."

That, my friend, is not building up. That crusty old man who thought he knew so much was evidently ignorant (or willfully ignorant) of Paul's words in Ephesians: "Do not let any unwholesome talk come out of your mouths, *but only what is helpful for building others up according to their needs,* that it may benefit those who listen" (4:29 NIV, emphasis added).

You never forget critical remarks like that. They tend to replay in your head during times of discouragement. When I was a young preacher, my wife and I visited a church in Cleveland, Ohio, where I had been asked to speak. In those days, they tried to squeeze as much out of the visiting preacher as they could, so they asked me to sing a solo before I preached my message.

Afterward, a lady came up to me and said, "I've heard you preach quite a bit. Son, you need to sing more." I hope she meant well by that. But I have to tell you, the remark left me speechless. I was so devastated by those words I didn't know what to do. You and I can be so adept at tearing down, can't we? We're demolition experts. We know where to swing the hammer. We know where to apply the crowbar. We know where to lay that charge of dynamite. Yet tearing down is the polar opposite of our calling in Scripture.

You say, "Where do you get that principle, anyway?" Please take a close look at these verses: "All things are lawful for me, but not all things are helpful; all things are lawful for me, but all things do not edify. Let no one seek his own, but each one the other's well-being" (1 Corinthians 10:23–24).

Paul is saying, "There are many things I might do and many things I might say. But my first concern ought not to be me. My first concern ought to be, will this build up or tear down my brother or sister in the body?"

That's the emphasis in God's Word: Build the church! Don't get sidetracked into areas that benefit only yourself.

First Thessalonians 5:11 says, "Therefore comfort each other and edify one another, just as you also are doing." You can edify yourself, to some degree; but God's overarching plan is that we edify one another. I need your help and you need mine. I have gifts that benefit you; you have gifts that bless and benefit me. I hold you accountable to keep you from stumbling and you do the same for me.

That has to be our emphasis as we move into the unexplored territory of this new millennium. Believe me, nobody "out there" in the secular world is going to build us up. We'd better be busy doing it in our local fellowships and in our small groups and with our believing friends.

Every word that leaves our mouths ought to be spoken with careful regard to those who will hear them. It is not about me. It's about the saints.

It's Not What You Profess; It's What You Pursue

When it comes to people, are you a builder or a demolition expert? Most people would reply, "Oh, I'm a builder. Absolutely. I'm a positive person. I don't want to tear others down."

Yet people-building is something you have to work at. It isn't easy. It takes thought—and discipline. I am amazed how quickly I can slip into a spirit of sarcasm or cynicism (especially when I'm weary) with my staff at church or at home with my family. I've been asking the Lord to rid me of that tendency. Truthfully, I cannot think of any good use for sarcasm. Sometimes when you're in a comfortable environment with buddies and friends, you can get to tossing remarks back and forth—he zings you, you zing him right back, and it's all in "good fun." Right?

Yet you never know—sometimes people weigh your words, even words spoken in jest, much more heavily than you think they do. Maybe a month or two later you learn that some off-the-top remark you made stuck in someone's heart. You were "just kidding," but the remark pushed on a sore spot—it *hurt.* And that hurt may begin to fester.

It's easy to tear people down in a jesting, offhand sort of way. It's something we do in our culture. If we don't feel secure in where we are, we think we can climb up on somebody else's failure. Yet the Bible tells us, "Therefore let us pursue the things which make for peace and the things by which one may edify another. Do not destroy the work of God" (Romans 14:19–20).

Did you hear that? Let us *pursue* those things. Let's *go after* them. The New International Version says, "Let us therefore *make every effort* to do what leads to peace and to mutual edification." In other words, we have to do it *intentionally*. It won't happen accidentally. You don't get up one morning and float through the day edifying everyone you pass. You have to be on your knees before God, asking Him to fill you with His Spirit. You have to ask Him to show you opportunities. You have to be filled with the Word of God and begin to see people as individuals who need to be built up. And then you have to follow through and really do it! Good intentions benefit no one.

One of my favorite recreations over the last few years has been watching the San Diego Padres. I can sit there in Qualcomm Stadium, munch on a hot dog, and forget all my worries and pressures for a while. One of the things that amazes me as I watch these professional players is their concentration. Have you ever watched an outfielder diving for a line drive, just inside the foul line? It's poetry in motion. With his eye on that little ball hurtling toward him at great speed, he stretches out and puts himself in position to make the catch—sometimes sacrificing his body in the process.

That's the way it is when you pursue some spiritual goal like edifying fellow believers. It takes concentration. It takes focus. Sometimes you have to fight off the inevitable distractions and interruptions. Paul wrote to young Timothy, "As I urged you when I went into Macedonia—remain in Ephesus that you may charge some that they teach no other doctrine, nor give heed to fables and endless genealogies, which cause disputes rather than godly edification which is in faith" (1 Timothy 1:3–4).

It's easy to get sidetracked, isn't it? I get letters every week from people wanting me to become involved in a variety of programs, commissions, projects, boards, and tasks. I try to read these queries with a good heart. The truth is, I could get caught up in this issue or that issue, this righteous cause or that righteous cause, to the point that that's all I would be doing. But you see, I am only one person and I can't concentrate on a great number of things at one time. I have to look at all these questions through the grid of what God has called me to do. God has called me to teach the Word of God and build people up through His truth. If I expend all my energy marching, disputing, and sitting on commissions, I won't be able to pursue what God has called me to pursue.

All of us face myriad challenges, options, and choices. We have to sit down and intentionally say, "No, I can't do that. Not because I don't want to, but because I have to say no to that so I can say yes to this."

I'm reminded of a word I found not long ago: *posteriorities.* Isn't that a great word? "Posteriorities" is the opposite of "priorities." "Posteriorities" are all the things you are *not* going to do, in the order in which you are not going to do them! Isn't that a wonderful thought? If you want to pursue peace and things that build up fellow believers, you have to have quite a list of "posteriorities."

That's what Paul was saying to Timothy: Don't get involved in all that stuff. Don't get tangled up in endless controversies and divisive, pointless arguments. Get involved in the things that will build up the body of Christ. Use that as your grid, as you make decisions about your daily calendar. Does it build up men and women? Does it edify the church? If not . . . do I really have time for it?

In one of his books on the family, Patrick Morley described being cornered one day by an angry acquaintance. "I tried to call you the other night, but you have an *unlisted* phone number!"

"Yes," he replied.

"Well, I had important ministry business that I wanted to discuss with you. I can't believe you have an unlisted phone number! How can you be a Christian and have an unlisted phone number?"

"It's real easy," Morley said. "All you do is call the phone company, tell them what you want, and they take care of everything."

But then he added, "Look, I'm willing to die for you until 6:00 P.M. But after 6:00 P.M., I only die for my family. And the only way to know that we will have time for our family is to put it on the schedule like any other appointment. I would rather be a nobody in the world and be a somebody to my kids."[1]

That's focus, my friend. That's pursuing the building up of his family. And it's hard work! It may be the hardest work we do. If you want to be a builder, you have to start out with that as your purpose and say, "By God's grace, by His enabling power, I will be one who builds. I will not be one who tears down."

It's Not How Much You Know; It's How Much You Care

First Corinthians 8:1 says, "Now about food sacrificed to idols: We know that we all possess knowledge. *Knowledge puffs up, but love builds up*" (NIV, emphasis added).

Edification isn't about how smart you are. It's not about how many courses you have taken in school, how many seminary classes you have under your belt, or how many impressive books you've read. Edification starts primarily in the heart when you open your eyes, see people you care about, and find ways to love and encourage them.

When you've been wounded yourself, you begin to see wounded people in a new light. You find yourself with an entirely different attitude toward hurting people. My bouts with cancer have forever changed the way I view people in pain. And that's precisely what Paul said would happen in his second letter to the Corinthians:

Thank God, the Father of our Lord Jesus Christ, that he is our Father and the source of all mercy and comfort. For he gives us comfort in all our trials so that we in turn may be able to give the same sort of strong sympathy to others in their troubles that we receive from God. Indeed, experience shows that the more we share in Christ's immeasurable suffering the more we are able to give of his encouragement. (2 Corinthians 1:3–5 PHILLIPS)

Sharing the encouragement of Jesus has little to do with head knowledge and everything to do with the inclination of the heart.

It's Not About Your Gifts; It's About Your Goals

I'm glad for the books and seminars and tests that help people identify their spiritual gifts. I believe everyone has a gift and ought to be aware of it and how to put it to work. But once you have that nailed down, *don't forget what the gift is for.*

Some treat their spiritual gifts like my grandson treats his soccer ball. He thinks that ball is the center of his universe. Whenever he sees me, he says "ball," because I play ball with him whenever he is around. Whenever he looks through a magazine and sees something round, he says, "ball." Not long ago he saw a huge water tank in a Florida city and he said, "ball." Sometimes I think the boy has a one-track mind. Of course his father and his grandfather know he is just getting started toward an all-American career.

As he gets older he will discover that it is really hard to play soccer by yourself, and you really need someone with more skill than your grandfather. He will learn that soccer or baseball or football is a team game and that real joy comes in pursuing the goal of winning as a part of a team.

Unfortunately some Christians never do learn that lesson about the Christian life. They view their spiritual gifts as if they were for their own use and enjoyment. They never seem to understand that the greatest sense of fulfillment as a believer is to see how God is using his spiritual gift to enhance the body of Christ and build up a winning team for His honor and glory.

The apostle really takes off the gloves in two passages speaking to this matter. He leaves no doubt where he stands. In 1 Corinthians 14:12, he says: "Even so you, since you are zealous for spiritual gifts, let it be for the edification of the church that you seek to excel." That's pretty plain, isn't it? You don't have to look that verse up in a commentary to understand what he means.

Later in the chapter he writes: "How is it then, brethren? Whenever you come together, each of you has a psalm, has a teaching, has a tongue, has a revelation, has an interpretation. Let all things be done for edification" (1 Corinthians 14:26). Paul was saying, "When you get together, folks, don't be so consumed with how you're going to exercise this or that gift. It's not your gift that's important, it's your goal with that gift. What are you doing with it?"

The gift itself ought to be incidental. A person ought not to be running around telling everyone what his or her gift is. Can you imagine a man at a building site, running around with a big, shiny hammer, telling all the builders how gifted he is with that hammer, how well he scored in hammering tests, and how fulfilled he feels whenever he picks up that hammer? How silly! If you bring a hammer to the building site, start driving some nails. And if there aren't any nails to pound, set down that hammer and pick up a saw. Or start carrying bundles of shingles up to the roof. Or pick up the trash. Just get busy. Why? Because there is a building to be erected and time may be short.

There is no time for self-centered preoccupation with gifting. In this hostile culture where believers get torn down just walking out their front doors, we need to pour all our energies into building up the body of Christ. It is all about the goal. It's not about the gift.

It's Not About Your Wisdom; It's About His Word

How do we know where to start this important process? Where do you place that first board or drive that first nail? How can you make sure you're more involved in the building process than you were last year or the year before that?

You may be asking yourself, "How am I going to turn this around? I know I've been negative. I know I say things I shouldn't and sometimes tear people down. I've done it for years. What can I do?"

Don't feel like the Lone Ranger, friend. As I already mentioned, I fight my own running battle with sarcasm and biting remarks. Our culture is permeated with it. It's what's in the news. It's a habit of life for millions of people you rub shoulders with every day. And it's the easiest thing in the world to get caught up in that current and just drift along with it, speaking and behaving like everyone else.

Where do I learn how to be a better builder? One of my favorite scenes in all the New Testament is Paul's encounter with the Ephesian elders on the beach at Miletus. Knowing he would never see these men again, he left them with this counsel: "And now, brethren, I commend you to God and to the word of His grace, which is able to build you up and give you an inheritance among all those who are sanctified" (Acts 20:32).

How do you get built up to the point that you can build up somebody else?

My friends, you need the Book.

Read the Bible. Study it. Memorize it. Meditate on it. If you are not spending time in the Word of God, I can almost promise you, you will tear down your own life—and tend to tear down the lives of others in turn. The Word of God is the fuel to help you be a builder. That is how you build yourself up, so that you in turn may build into the lives of others (Jude 20–21).

Let's Please the Master Builder

We need one another. We need one another's strength, help, encouragement, wisdom, warnings, and counsel. The growing hostility of our culture and the wholesale demolition of our nation's formerly godly foundations ought to drive us together as never before.

What should we be doing as we await His coming? We should be building one another up.

As His people, we are to lift one another up through prayer, share our material means, and go out of our way to offer heart-to-heart friendship and a genuine effort to meet one another's needs.

Scripture says, "Edify." Build the house.

And while you're busy building in someone else's life, you will find your own life being repaired, restored, and remodeled.

The Master Builder sees it all . . . and is well pleased!

Nine

———— ⟆⟅⟆ ————

PURSUE YOUR REWARD
UNTIL I COME

When our children were little, we used to load the whole Jeremiah tribe into the station wagon every year for a family vacation. We always enjoyed family together times, but as young parents, Donna and I became distressed by the constant squabbles in the backseats.

If you're a parent, you know exactly what I mean. We wouldn't be many miles down the road before unhappy voices—charges and countercharges, wails and weeping—began ricocheting into the front seat.

"Are we there yet?"

"I gotta go *bad*, Daddy."

"How much farther?"

"No, that's mine! You can't have it! Mom, make him leggo!"

"I got to sit by the window last time, and I'm gonna sit by the window this time too."

"He touched my elbow!"

"She *breathed* on me!"

All that sort of thing—and a thousand variations. After a while, those skirmishes in the backseat began to steal some of the joy from those family excursions.

Then my resourceful wife came up with an ingenious program. I'll never forget the first day she put it into operation. Vacations, after that day, were never the same.

We were packing the car for a cross-country trip when she called all the kids into the living room and lined 'em up. Then she reached into her purse and pulled out some rolls of coins—rolls of quarters for the older kids and rolls of dimes for the younger ones. She handed out the booty to our children, who stared wide-eyed at their sudden wealth.

This, Donna explained to them, was their spending money for the entire vacation. But before they could let loose with a cheer, she added her one condition. She would retain the prerogative to retrieve money *back* from them—a coin at a time—when they did not behave as instructed in the car.

Of course the kids had to test the system. Would Mom really enforce such conditions?

Yes, as a matter of fact, she would. We hadn't gone very far before I heard her say to one of the younger ones, "Okay, you owe me a dime. Hand it over."

"*What?*" The little voice was incredulous. "What do you mean?"

"You know very well what I mean. Remember our agreement? Give me a dime. Now."

So one dime returned (most reluctantly) to her purse. After that, it wasn't long before a few quarters started coming over the front seat.

And then . . . things began to change. We found out in a very short period of time who the real family entrepreneurs were. It became evident who cared most about hanging on to those coins. At least two of the children radically changed their whole mentality about what they would say and do in the car. I had never heard those two so quiet and calm in my whole life. They turned a blind eye to offenses and refused to be provoked. They were determined to beat the system and keep that money!

Yes, the Jeremiah family found the secret to tranquillity in travel. It's called "rewards"! Truthfully, Donna and I were the ones who reaped the benefits. Peace and harmony prevailed in the family wagon as never before.

Did you know that rewards are a major part of God's plan for His kids too? I know many people—godly people—who feel uncomfortable even discussing this issue. They reason, I suppose, that even thinking about future rewards displays a wrong or lesser motivation. *We ought to work hard and stay pure and lay down our lives out of love for the Lord alone,* they think.

I understand what they mean, but the Bible shows no such timidity. In fact, Scripture is *filled* with truth about rewards! And it doesn't blush to speak of them in the context of our motivations.

Bottom line, God rewards His servants. He is pleased and delighted to do so, and I believe a careful study of Scripture reveals that He *wants* us to be motivated by considering those rewards.

Heaven's Reward System

Through the pages of this book, we have considered our Lord's final warnings—His words of hope and encouragement as we step into a new millennium. One of those wonderful challenges appears near the end of the Bible's final book. The Lord Jesus says: "Behold, I am coming quickly, and My reward is with Me, to give to every one according to his work" (Revelation 22:12).

When the classic historian Gibbon sought to determine why Christianity flourished during the days of Roman rule, he came up with five major reasons:

1. The zeal of the early Christians
2. Their belief in future rewards

3. The power of miracles
4. The pure morals of Christians
5. The compact church organization

Did you catch number two on Gibbon's list? This historian said one of the principal reasons believers enjoyed such success during the ascendancy of Rome was *their strong belief in future rewards.*

Since we began this study together, we've heard our Lord Jesus urging us toward action as we await His return. He has told us, "Do business until I come. Evangelize. Edify. Work, for the night is coming!" God in no way wants His people sitting around, caught up in the nuances and details and timing of Christ's return. He wants us to be busy. And in order to energize us in the service of the King, He has put a system of rewards into place. We ought to carefully consider those rewards. In fact, it would please Him if we did.

As a young boy growing up in my father's church, I remember how Sunday school attendance awards used to be a big deal. Do you remember them? If you came to Sunday school so many weeks without missing, you got a pin to wear on your shirt or dress or jacket. And then every so often after that, you could win additional pins by hanging in there week after week.

You could look around the church and see those things gleaming on people's clothing. Some of those chains of pins got so long you began to wonder if someone would trip over them on the way to church. I remember people who really got into the display mode, parading their medals like a retired Russian general.

I'm sure there must have been Sundays when they felt lousy and didn't want to go to church, but hey—when you've got a five-and-a-half-year string going, you don't want to wimp out just because you're sick. So these people would drag themselves to church any-way—and infect everybody else!

The rewards of heaven, however, go infinitely beyond stickpins or rolls of quarters and dimes. In fact, even though we might list Bible verses by the score, we can never really understand in this life how wonderful and desirable those heavenly rewards will be. As Paul wrote: *"No eye has seen, no ear has heard, no mind has conceived what God has prepared for those who love him"* (1 Corinthians 2:9 NIV, emphasis added).

Even so, it is good for us to focus on these verses. Listen to some of these biblical statements that describe God's system of rewards.

And men will say, "Surely there is a reward for the righteous; surely there is a God who judges on earth!" (Psalm 58:11 NASB)

You, O Lord, are loving. Surely you will reward each person according to what he has done. (Psalm 62:12 NIV)

When we come to the New Testament, it's obvious that the Lord Jesus frequently spoke about rewards to His disciples.

For whoever gives you a cup of water to drink in My name, because you belong to Christ, assuredly, I say to you, he will by no means lose his reward. (Mark 9:41)

Assuredly, I say to you, there is no one who has left house or brothers or sisters or father or mother or wife or children or lands, for My sake and the gospel's, who shall not receive a hundredfold now in this time—houses and brothers and sisters and mothers and children and lands, with persecutions—and in the age to come, eternal life. (Mark 10:29–30)

Rejoice and be exceedingly glad, for great is your reward in heaven, for so they persecuted the prophets who were before you. (Matthew 5:12)

The book of Hebrews gives us these strongly motivational words:

For God is not unjust to forget your work and labor of love which you have shown toward His name, in that you have ministered to the saints, and do minister. And we desire that each one of you show the same diligence to the full assurance of hope until the end, that you do not become sluggish, but imitate those who through faith and patience inherit the promises. (Hebrews 6:10–12)

You just can't read the Bible without bumping into rewards. "Yes," some will counter, "but the Bible isn't speaking about rewards as we understand them today. It means something totally different."

Totally different? I'm not so sure about that. Yes, these rewards will be beyond our comprehension—but certainly God wants us to understand enough so that we will be greatly motivated. Why else would He tell us?

Do you want to know the Hebrew meaning of "rewards"?

It's REWARDS.

What does the word say in the Greek?

It says REWARDS.

The Bible isn't referring to some mystical concept beyond our grasp. When it says rewards, it means *rewards*. Payment for something done. Something delightful and desirable presented for services rendered.

Of course, it doesn't mean something *owed*. It doesn't mean fair wages. It doesn't mean you get paid ten dollars an hour for a job that's worth ten dollars an hour. No, it's more like winning the Publisher's Clearing House ten million dollar sweepstakes. Does the winner ever *earn* that money? No. But does he have to qualify to receive it? Yes. Does he have to follow the rules and do what the instructions tell him to do in order to win? Yes. Does filling out the forms and sending them in on time *earn* the winner his money? Has he done enough work to be owed all that money? Clearly, no. But what he did qualified him for the prize, a prize hugely out of proportion to the labor he expended.

That's what the Bible means by rewards.

The New Testament speaks of a very well-defined system; after the rapture of the church, God will reward His people. One of the first events that will take place in heaven after the Rapture is the judgment seat of Christ, or the *bema,* where all believers will stand before the Lord. This will not be to determine where we will spend eternity. That subject won't even come up, because it will have already been decided. At the bema, you and I will stand before our Lord and be judged with a view to rewards.

The Bible tells us that after the church is taken to heaven, either by rapture or by the resurrection, individual believers will be judged for their works done in the body as Christians. At that time, special rewards will be handed out.

This is not only the clear teaching of the New Testament, it is one of the apostle Paul's favorite doctrines. For instance, in Romans 14:10 we read, "But why do you judge your brother? Or why do you show contempt for your brother? For we shall all stand before the judgment seat of Christ."

Who is going to stand before the judgment seat of Christ? A brother. A Christian. The bema is not for nonbelievers.

In 2 Corinthians 5:10 we read again, "For we must all appear before the judgment seat of Christ, that each one may receive the things done in the body, according to what he has done, whether good or bad."

In 1 Corinthians chapter 3, which is the central passage on this truth, we read these amazing words:

> For no other foundation can anyone lay than that which is laid, which is Jesus Christ. Now if anyone builds on this foundation with gold, silver, precious stones, wood, hay, straw, each one's work will become clear; for the Day will declare it, because it will be revealed by fire; and the fire will test each one's work, of what sort it is. If anyone's work which he has built on it endures, he will receive a reward. If anyone's work is burned, he will suffer loss; *but he himself will be saved, yet so as through fire.* (vv. 11–15, emphasis added)

Now let me set the stage a little. The Bible tells us there will be two major judgments in the future. The first is the one we just looked at, the judgment seat of Christ. This takes place in heaven during the time of the tribulation on earth, immediately following the Rapture.

Then, after the thousand-year reign of Christ upon the earth is complete, there will be the judgment at the Great White Throne. At that time (terrible to contemplate!) nonbelievers will be judged for their sin and their rejection of God's grace and salvation in Christ.

Don't confuse these two events! Not a single nonbeliever will stand before the judgment seat of Christ. The judgment of nonbelievers will be reserved for the Great White Throne later on.

This text we have been considering, 1 Corinthians 3:11–15, is one of the most misunderstood passages in all of the Bible. Our Catholic friends, for instance, use this passage as a basis for their doctrine of purgatory. They teach that fire will purify people in the next life and make them fit for heaven. Our modernist friends cite this passage as evidence that a person achieves heaven by virtue of his good works. If he performs enough of them, he gets through the fire, and if he doesn't . . . (But I can't help wondering, how much is *enough?*)

Both have completely misunderstood the meaning and context of this passage. Let me begin by showing what this passage does *not* say.

This Is Not About Judgment of the Believer's Sin

Let me tell you why I know that. The Bible tells us that judgment already took place. It's over! When was your sin judged? It was judged at the cross of Jesus Christ. Your sins will not be judged, because God already poured out the full fury of His judgment and wrath on Jesus Christ as He hung there on the cross, between heaven and earth, on our behalf.

Christ was condemned for us. Galatians 1:3–4 tells us that "our

Lord Jesus Christ . . . gave Himself for our sins, that He might deliver us from this present evil age." Paul says it again in 1 Corinthians 15:3: "For I delivered to you first of all that which I also received: that Christ died for our sins according to the Scriptures." Peter adds his amen in 1 Peter 2:24: "Who Himself bore our sins in His own body on the tree."

Scripture tells us over and over that Christ took the penalty of our sin—all of it—upon Himself. If you put your trust in Christ, you do not have to pay that penalty, because *it has already been paid in full*. Colossians 2:13 says, "And you, being dead in your trespasses and the uncircumcision of your flesh, He has made alive together with Him, having forgiven you *all trespasses*" (emphasis added).

God has no more charges against you. Isn't that glorious news? Maybe you remember the old hymn that says it so well:

My sin—O the bliss of this glorious thought,
My sin—not in part but the whole,
Is nailed to the cross and I bear it no more,
Praise the Lord, praise the Lord, O my soul!

Romans 8:1 says, "There is therefore now no condemnation to those who are in Christ Jesus." You will never face your sin again.

People ask me, "But Pastor Jeremiah, how can someone have his sins forgiven and still have his works reviewed at the judgment seat of Christ? Don't those ideas seem to be in conflict?"

No, because forgiveness is about justification, and rewards are about the things we do as justified people. These are not works done *for* justification; they are works done *as* a justified person.

One of the greatest truths about Scripture that I have learned through the years is the concept of *biblical tension*. God has put the Word together in such a way that if we read it carefully, we will not veer off to the left or the right, to this extreme or that extreme. For instance, one of the great truths about a Christian is that we are saved by faith, not by works. Ephesians 2:8–9 says, "For by grace you have been saved through faith, and that not of yourselves; it is the gift of God, not of works, lest anyone should boast."

Now, most people stop right there. But the passage goes on: "For we are His workmanship, created in Christ Jesus for good works, which God prepared beforehand that we should walk in them" (v. 10).

Do you see that? What Paul said to the Ephesians was this: "You can't do enough works to get saved. But when you become a Christian, it is apparent that the very purpose for which God has saved you is so that you might live your life as an open testimony and do good works for His glory."

The issue before the judgment seat of Christ will be the works we have done *after* salvation. Someday you are going to stand before the mighty Son of God "whose eyes are like blazing fire" (Revelation 2:18 NIV), and He will walk you through a review of your life as a believer. And the issue at that time will be rewards.

Bible history and church history, as you know, are filled with people who began the race with great eagerness and determination, but in the end they became careless, disregarded God's rules, and wandered off the track. While these people did not lose their salvation, they lost the joy of being a faithful servant of almighty God. I think of people like Lot, Samson, and Ananias and Sapphira. And remember what Paul wrote of the brother named Demas? "Do your best to come to me quickly, for Demas, because he loved this world, has deserted me and has gone to Thessalonica" (2 Timothy 4:9–10 NIV). You and I can hardly help but think of contemporaries who walked away from their families or ministries for all the wrong reasons. They, along with us, must give an account of their service before Jesus Christ.

With that thought in mind, however, there is another truth we must remember about 1 Corinthians 3:11–15.

This Is Not About One Believer's Judgment of Another Believer

We're quick to judge. Some people regard it as a favorite indoor sport. Yet we ought to constantly remind ourselves that God has not called any of us to judge anyone else. Because *all* believers must stand before the judgment seat of Christ, every one of us giving account of himself to God, we have no right to judge the work or the motives of other believers.

When it comes right down to it, you really don't know my motives, do you? Nor do I know yours. You can't see my heart of hearts, and I can't see yours. We may form our opinions along the way, but I can promise you this: There will be a great many surprises at the judgment seat of Christ. You can count on it!

First Corinthians 4:5 offers a timely warning: "Therefore judge nothing before the appointed time; wait till the Lord comes. He will bring to light what is hidden in darkness and will expose the motives of men's hearts. At that time each will receive his praise from God" (NIV).

What a great reminder that it is not our job to judge others. The Lord says, "You leave that to Me."

I have sat through a number of award ceremonies. There have been times when I thought, for one reason or another, I might be a candidate for one of the awards. Then someone else got it. In a moment like that, you can't help reviewing a bit: *Well, if I had done a little more of this and worked a little harder at that, perhaps I could have received that award.*

That is the sort of review that will take place when each of us stands before our Lord and our lives are brought under review. Does that thought make you uncomfortable? Does it make you want to reflect on your life just a little and think through some of your thoughts and actions? It ought to! In fact, we ought to live every day of our lives with eternity in view.

It was said of Jonathan Edwards that he enjoyed walking slowly along garden pathways, praying and meditating. Sometimes he would stop, perhaps pick up some little clear stone he found on the ground, and look through it at the sunlight. Children thought he was eccentric and would ask him what he was doing. Edwards would simply reply that he was thinking about heaven. One day somebody said the problem with Jonathan Edwards was that he had eternity stamped in his eyeballs.

When I read those words, I thought, *I should have such a problem!* What a way for a person to go through life! So often you and I have the world stamped on our eyeballs. But Jonathan Edwards saw life from a different perspective. I believe that we, too, will begin to see life from a new point of view as we ponder our Lord's words: "Behold, I am coming quickly, and My reward is with Me" (Revelation 22:12).

Five Crowns

Let's take a few moments to survey five of the rewards mentioned in the New Testament.

1. The Crown of the Victor
In 1 Corinthians 9:25–27, Paul writes:

Everyone who competes in the games goes into strict training. They do it to get a crown that will not last; but we do it to get a crown that will last forever. Therefore I do not run like a man running aimlessly; I do not fight like a man beating the air. No, I beat my body and make it my slave so that after I have preached to others, I myself will not be disqualified for the prize. (NIV)

The apostle speaks here about an imperishable crown, a crown that will last forever. "This," says Paul, "is the crown I'm going after." He uses a word picture that would have been very compelling to that particular group of believers. The Corinthians had two great athletic events in their time, the Olympic Games and the Isthmian Games. The Isthmian Games were held in Corinth. So this would have been like Paul writing to New Yorkers and making reference to the Yankees team—or talking to Green Bay folks about their Packers. Paul had their attention!

Contestants in those games had to rigorously train for ten months. The last month was spent in Corinth, where contestants were supervised daily in the gymnasium and on the athletic fields. The race was always a major attraction at the games; that is the figure Paul used to illustrate the faithful Christian life. Many may run in this race, he said, but only one receives the prize. No one would train so hard and so long without intending to win. Yet out of the large number of runners in the Isthmian Games, only one would win.

The Isthmian athletes worked diligently for a long time to gain an insignificant prize. Paul's thought was, "How much more should we as Christians take control of our bodies, take control of our energies, take control of our motives and our purposes, and discipline ourselves so that we can be useful servants of God!" The man or woman who does that is a candidate for the imperishable crown, the victor's crown.

In the Isthmian Games, the prize was a simple pine wreath wrapped around the head. Contestants wanted that wreath because honor went with the award. But that honor was just as perishable as the wreath itself. The cheers and recognition and fame and sense of accomplishment faded all too quickly.

In contrast, Peter reminds us that we have "an inheritance incorruptible and undefiled . . . that does not fade away, reserved in heaven for [us], who are kept by the power of God through faith for salvation ready to be revealed in the last time" (1 Peter 1:4–5).

You ask, "How does this 'victor's crown' work in everyday life? How do we pursue it today?" I can think of a number of practical ways. It begins by taking control of your humanity through the Spirit of God, making sure you are not pouring all your time and energies into pursuing temporal fame or material possessions, but rather disciplining your body for an eternal goal. Like Edwards of old, we allow the Spirit of God to stamp eternity on our eyeballs and begin to look at life through those lenses, not allowing the world to squeeze us into its own mold.

At the bema seat of Christ, earthly wreaths and trophies and newspaper clippings and Super Bowl rings will be long forgotten. They'll be no more important than brushing your teeth or buying a newspaper at the corner store. But what we do for eternity—even the smallest of deeds—will count forever.

You and I have a chance to win this victor's crown, and it is infinitely worth the effort. When we make the choice to put God first, no matter what, when we use our energies for His purposes, we are reaching for that beautiful crown.

2. The Crown of Rejoicing

This second reward has been called the soul winner's crown. First Thessalonians 2:19 tells us: "For what is our hope, or joy, or crown of rejoicing? Is it not even you in the presence of our Lord Jesus Christ at His coming?"

There will be a crown given to those who take a lot of people to heaven with them. Through the years I have met a number of individuals who never ceased winning people to Jesus Christ. It was their passion, their delight, their reason for getting up in the morning. And when we meet these people in heaven someday, we will know them by this radiant crown of rejoicing. And who wouldn't rejoice as you look around heaven and see men and women and children whom you had the privilege of introducing to the Savior? These are the ones who will welcome you "into eternal dwellings" (Luke 16:9 NIV).

3. The Crown of Righteousness

Perhaps you have been through some rugged, even tragic experiences over the last few months and years. You have endured some difficult days—and more and more, you have treasured the hope of Christ's return. You have kept watch out of the corner of your eye, realizing that He might come at any moment to call us into the clouds to meet Him. Scripture says there is a special reward for those "who have loved His appearing": "Finally, there is laid up for me the crown of righteousness, which the Lord, the righteous Judge, will give to me on that Day, and not to me only but also to all who have loved His appearing" (2 Timothy 4:8).

There will be a crown given to those who look forward to our Lord's return. Frankly, I don't see many people doing that these days. It isn't fashionable or chic to talk about the Second Coming. When I was a boy, I remember how people used to say to one another, "It may be today!" or "Maybe tonight." So many these days are caught up in the details of the present age: politics, the stock market, making money, and recreating on the weekends. We aren't longing for His return because we're too busy living life in the fast lane. Nevertheless, our Lord has reserved special recognition for those who watch and long for His return.

4. The Crown of Life

James 1:12 says, "Blessed is the man who endures temptation [testing]; for when he has been proved, he will receive the crown of life which the Lord has promised to those who love Him."

The book of Revelation adds these words: "Do not fear any of those things which you are about to suffer. Indeed, the devil is about to throw some of you into prison, that you may be tested, and you will have tribulation ten days. Be faithful until death, and I will give you the crown of life" (2:10).

Even as you read these words, believing men, women, and children are enduring humiliation, deprivation, bitter persecution, and even death for their faith in the Lord Jesus. It's happening *today* in China, in Indonesia, in India, in the Sudan, and all over the world. These dear brothers and sisters will also stand before the judgment seat of Christ—and our Lord will not overlook their suffering. Each will be crowned with an unspeakably beautiful crown of life—the martyr's crown—because they paid for their faith with their very lives.

5. *The Crown of Glory*

This final crown will be presented to faithful pastors and leaders. Peter wrote: "And when the Chief Shepherd appears, you will receive the crown of glory that does not fade away" (1 Peter 5:4). There is a unique crown for those who faithfully teach the Word of God and shepherd God's people—an activity so near and dear to the Great Shepherd's heart. If we are steadfast in pouring out our lives for those under our care, God will provide us with an unfading, eternal crown.

Whenever you hear this doctrine of rewards taught, my friend, always reject the two common misconceptions about rewards. First, remember that righteousness is not always rewarded materially here on this earth; and second, remember that suffering is not a certain sign of sin. Don't fall into the trap of Job's accusers and earn God's stern rebuke as they did!

The Lord Himself Is Your Chief Reward

As Abraham returned from defeating the pagan kings, he was met by the grateful king of Sodom, who sought to reward the patriarch. Abraham steadfastly refused, telling this godless ruler, "I have lifted my hand to the LORD, God Most High, the Possessor of heaven and earth, that I will take nothing, from a thread to a sandal strap, and that I will not take anything that is yours, lest you should say, 'I have made Abram rich'" (Genesis 14:22–23).

Abraham was saying, "Man, I don't want so much as a shoelace. Keep the stuff yourself." Then, in the very next verse after Abraham's reply, the Lord appears to him and says, "Do not be afraid, Abram. I am your shield, your exceedingly great reward" (Genesis 15:1).

In other words, "You made the right choice, son. You rejected the earthly king's booty, and now I, the King of the universe, will reward you with everything that I am."

We may not be enriched or rewarded or acknowledged for our efforts through the days of our lives. But oh my friend, a day is coming! The Lord who misses nothing will reward us with the beauty and glory and nearness of His presence through endless ages. There can be no better reward than God Himself.

Resist Doing Works for Earthly Reward

Remember what the Lord Jesus says in Matthew 6:1, 3–4: "Take heed that you do not do your charitable deeds before men, to be seen by them. Otherwise you have no reward from your Father in heaven. . . . When you do a charitable deed, do not let your left hand know what your right hand is doing, that your charitable deed may be in secret; and your Father who sees in secret will Himself reward you openly."

So while we concern ourselves with working for eternal rewards, we don't want to spoil it all by angling for earthly recognition. You don't want to parade yourself in front of folks, reminding them, "I did this . . ." or, "No one knows about it, but I did that." The Bible says if you do that, you get your reward here—yet you may miss the one there! What a terrible exchange that would be. I'd much rather hold out for the one on the other side, because there really is no comparison. Maybe you and I should get just a little bit pragmatic here and hold out for the *really* good one!

How do you do that? To begin with, don't go around broadcasting all your good works. Don't position yourself to receive compliments or recognition—even though you may crave it. There are better rewards on the other side.

Reflect on the Ultimate Goal of Rewards

What are we going to do with these crowns and rewards after we receive them? The apostle John gives us a good picture in Revelation 4:10–11:

> The twenty-four elders fall down before Him who sits on the throne and worship Him who lives forever and ever, and cast their crowns before the throne, saying: "You are worthy, O Lord, to receive glory and honor and power; for You created all things, and by Your will they exist and were created."

What a scene! And what an awesome day that will be! When that day comes, I don't want to be empty-handed. I want to have something with which I, too, can honor my Lord and Savior, who redeemed me with His own blood. I want to be able to say to Him, "Lord God, I could never repay You for what You have done for me, but I want to lay this crown at Your feet, in token of all You have done for me."

When that moment comes, I don't want to have to reflect and remember, *I had a chance in my life to live my life that way, and I took the other way.* Heaven is no place for regrets!

Pursue your reward till He comes, my friend. I can't even describe how much is at stake. This is no time to be idle or to allow ourselves to be caught up in peripheral matters that sap our energy and strength and desire.

Let's follow Jonathan Edwards and let people say we have eternity stamped on our eyeballs. Let's live for heaven, remembering that He could come with the next heartbeat . . . and remembering that the smile of His favor is worth everything, infinitely more than earth's best treasures.

Bert looked into time from heaven and saw the atrocities carried out in the human realm. Absolutely aghast, he pointed to one unspeakable scene and asked God about it, "How can You allow it? Look what evil is setting in motion down there!"

"There's no one better than the devil for creating a tragedy like that!" God said.

"But God, that man is one of Your people . . . oh, that poor man!"

"I gave the freedom to choose between good and evil," God said, His face sad. "No matter what they choose, they all live there together. Sometimes, those who choose My way are impacted by those who don't." He slowly shook His head. "It's always painful when that happens."

"But those people right there have no choice," Bert protested. "Evil is being crammed down their throats! That isn't a choice!"

"Now, Bert," God said patiently, "have I ever let pain go unavenged?"

"No . . . no, but . . ." Bert cringed from the sight, unable to bear any more.

"Watch!" God put His arm around Bert's hunched shoulders and turned him again. "Look right over there, by the wall."

"That one? He looks nearly dead. Is he praying?"

"Ah, Bert, you should hear his prayers!" Intense love flashed in God's eyes like lightning. "Simple prayers from an aching heart. *This* is triumph over evil. Trusting Me—*that* is the choice." God smiled through sparkling tears of love. "Isn't he magnificent?"

Together they stood in silence, and Bert began to see as God did.

"Now watch this, Bert." God spoke softly, never letting His eyes leave the scene. He called for Michael and the archangel appeared.

"Go down and get him, Michael." The tears of divine joy spilled over. "I'll arrange the party."[1]

Ten

LIVE IN HOPE UNTIL I COME

A single man in his middle years took a Caribbean cruise. On the first day at sea, he noticed an attractive woman about his own age who smiled at him when they passed each other on deck. That very day he went to the maître d' in the dining room and asked if he could be seated at this woman's table. The maître d' was glad to oblige.

Later that evening after the pair were seated, they began to converse and the man mentioned how he had first seen her on the deck that day and had appreciated very much her friendly smile.

The woman smiled again and said, "Well, the reason I smiled was that when I saw you, I was immediately struck by your strong resemblance to my third husband."

The man's ears pricked. "Oh?" he said. "How many times have you been married?"

The woman looked down at her plate and smiled again. "Twice," she answered.

Now, *that* is what you call hope!

Another seagoing passenger wasn't quite so blessed. In the middle of an extended pleasure cruise, the rocking and rolling of the ship made him violently seasick. One afternoon he was hanging over the edge of the ship, his face a shocking shade of pale green. A steward came along, saw him in his acute distress, and said kindly, "Don't be discouraged, sir. I just want you to know no one has ever died of sea-sickness."

The nauseated passenger looked up and groaned. "Oh, *please* don't say that," he replied. "It's only the hope of dying that has kept me alive *this* long."

The Necessity of Hope

Hope. Who among us can live without it?

A few years ago I read an article that cited an example given by Major F. J. Harold Cushner, an army medical officer during the Vietnam War who was held prisoner by the Vietcong for five and a half years. He told the *New York Magazine* about meeting a twenty-four-year-old marine who had already survived two years of prison camp.

The marine seemed to be in relatively good health and appeared to be doing fine. When Kushner asked him how he happened to be doing so well, the young man explained that the camp commander had promised him an early release if he cooperated in every respect. Because the marine had seen other prisoners granted such a gift, he agreed. He became a model prisoner and served as head of the camp's "thought reform group," which tried to brainwash other prisoners.

As time passed, however, it became clear to the marine that he had been lied to. When this realization finally hit home, the young man became a zombie. He refused all work and rejected all offers of food and encouragement. He simply lay on his cot, sucking his thumb, until a few days later he died. When his hope of release vanished, he found he had nothing left to live for.[1]

Jesus and Hope

I doubt our world has ever needed hope more than it does today. Just as Jesus prophesied so long ago, we see kingdom rising against kingdom and ethnic group against ethnic group. No one knows where scores of old Soviet nuclear weapons have vanished to; droughts and floods and earthquakes ravage the planet in increasing intensity; scandals in government and business rock the nations; and a major worldwide recession looks more and more probable. The ozone layer continues to shrink while weapons of mass destruction continue to proliferate. Secular authors write books with titles like *Slouching Toward Gomorrah* and *Judgment Day at the White House* while religious authors write *Wicca: A Guide for the Solitary Practitioner* and *Death of the Church.*

Because our world looks like this, Mike Bellah in his article titled "Make Room for Baby Boomers" has written,

> Baby boomers desperately need hope. The church that reaches this generation will be one where hope is frequently dispensed. However, it is important that the church offer real, not contrived, hope. The kind of hope promised by the success gospel is looked on with a deserved cynicism by most baby boomers. Similarly, the hope offered by sincere but unrealistic Christians, which ignores real pain and suffering, will not help disillusioned baby boomers. This generation will not respond to religious platitudes and clichés that minimize the hurt found in a fallen world. The church that offers hope to baby boomers will proclaim the God of Joseph, Daniel, Elijah and others like them. It will reveal a God who does not always remove us from our crises, but who supports us in them and brings us through them.[2]

Friend, we need some solid *hope!*

The disciples of our Lord felt a similar need as the time neared for Jesus to offer Himself as a sacrifice for our sins. They weren't quite sure what lay ahead, but they knew something big was up; a dark foreboding had settled on their hearts. Jesus knew all about their fears and so declared to them:

> Most assuredly, I say to you that you will weep and lament, but the world will rejoice; and you will be sorrowful, but your sorrow will be turned into joy. A woman, when she is in labor, has sorrow because her hour has come; but as soon as she has given birth to the child, she no longer remembers the anguish, for joy that a human being has been born into the world. Therefore you now have sorrow; but I will see you again and your heart will rejoice, and your joy no one will take from you. (John 16:20–22)

Most scholars believe Jesus' comments here refer to His imminent death and resurrection, but I believe they have application far beyond that. Although the Master doesn't use the word *hope* here, His prophetic words shout it aloud!

"Listen," He says to His men, "I know you're confused. I know you're worried and anxious. And I won't mislead you: Real and terrible pain lies ahead. But never allow the pain to obscure the hope! I am the Lord of hope, and I know how to bring joy out of sorrow."

The Lord's powerful ministry of hope was prophesied long before He walked this earth. The prophet Isaiah, especially, gloried in the storehouses of hope to be thrown open by the coming Messiah. "Those who hope in me will not be disappointed," he reports the Lord saying (Isaiah 49:23 NIV). "My righteousness draws near speedily, my salvation is on the way, and my arm will bring justice to the nations. The islands will look to me and wait in hope for my arm" (Isaiah 51:5 NIV).

In his Gospel, Matthew pointed to this prophetic emphasis on the hope Messiah was to bring. He tells us that the Lord "healed all their sick, warning them not to tell who he was," then adds,

This was to fulfill what was spoken through the prophet Isaiah: "Here is my servant whom I have chosen, the one I love, in whom I delight; I will put my Spirit on him, and he will proclaim justice to the nations. He will not quarrel or cry out; no one will hear his voice in the streets. A bruised reed he will not break, and a smoldering wick he will not snuff out, till he leads justice to victory. In his name the nations will put their hope." (Matthew 12:15–21 NIV, quoting Isaiah 42:1–4)

This was the message the disciples needed to hear in the anxious days leading up to the Crucifixion. And they especially needed to remember it in the crushing days immediately following the death of our Lord. "You now have sorrow," Jesus had told them, "but I will see you again and your heart will rejoice, and your joy no one will take from you" (John 16:22).

Never on this earth has there been a time when we haven't needed hope—but hope is critical when the ones we love the most are about to leave us. I believe that is why Jesus picked this time to fill His disciples with hope. Their Master and friend was about to leave them, they didn't understand the forces that were gathering to sweep Him away, and they needed to be assured that a rock-solid hope remained.

All of us have felt the emotional pain of saying good-bye to somebody we love. Perhaps we've lost a job. Or we've seen the breakup of a home, perhaps even our own. And the questions in all of our hearts are, "Where do I go? What do I do? Where can I find hope?" We feel as if we have been abandoned at the corner of Hopelessness and Despair.

The good news is that we who know God through His Son, Jesus Christ, don't have to be left at such a desperate corner. There *is* an answer, and His name is Jesus. That's not trite. It's not merely theological. It's not just church talk.

It's true.

Peter and Hope

In 1 Peter chapter 1, the apostle makes an important statement about the nature of our hope. Peter knew how important it was to dispense such hope to his readers. Not only did he recall the desperate time when his Lord was about to leave him, but he also knew the recipients of his little letter were enduring tremendous hardships.

These Christians, salted throughout the Roman Empire, lived at a time when Rome tyrannized believers. They faced untold persecution and suffering. In fact, Peter used the word *suffering* sixteen times in this five-chapter epistle.

Peter has a good word for us about how to face troubled times. That word is *hope.* He insists we can live in hope if we understand and believe the truth concerning the risen Christ. In 1 Peter 1:3 he says, "Blessed be the God and Father of our Lord Jesus Christ, who according to His abundant mercy has begotten us again to a living hope through the resurrection of Jesus Christ from the dead."

A living hope.

Peter would have us believe that the hope we seek and that so often seems to elude us (if we don't carefully listen to God's Word) is to be found in a Person who has overcome death.

I Remember When . . .

I wonder what was going through Peter's mind as he wrote these words. I can't help but think that when the apostle proclaimed a living hope in the resurrected Christ, his own personal experience rushed back into his mind in Technicolor and surround-sound.

Peter had been a very close friend of the Lord. He had walked with Him through most of His public ministry. Oh, it's true he'd had some problems. He denied the Lord and had to be recommissioned. That's why we all like Peter so much; he gives us a sense of identity. We believe that if *he* could make it with the Lord, maybe *we* can too.

But in the end, Peter loved the Lord and hoped that this Jesus was the One who would be their Messiah, who would free them from Roman bondage. Peter was like all the rest who had pinned their hope on Jesus.

Then one day it happened: the anger, the accusations, the mock trial, the beating, the crown of thorns, the cross, the journey up the hill, the nails, the spear, the darkness. And everything Peter had believed in, everything he had hoped for, was taken down from that cross, wrapped in linen, and laid in a cold, rock-hewn tomb.

If we could have looked into Peter's heart during the days between the death of Christ and His resurrection, I think we would have seen the epitome of hopelessness and despair. The Gospels make it clear that Peter was dumbfounded by what was happening. Shell-shocked.

Then on the third day, word started to filter down that friends had visited the tomb, looked inside—and found it empty. Had the body been stolen? But Peter was from Missouri. "Show me," he demanded. He wanted to see for himself. He ran to the tomb with John and when he stooped, looked in, and saw the Lord's garments by themselves, Scripture says the reality of the resurrection of Jesus Christ began to dawn in his heart.

And then came the moment when he saw the resurrected Lord Himself. He examined the nail prints in His hands and the place where the spear had pierced His side. It overwhelmed Peter to realize that this One whom he had seen die, go into the grave, and remain there for three days, had on the third day exploded from the tomb by His own power, victorious over man's greatest enemy. Jesus had come back from the dead. He was alive! He was the risen Lord!

So Peter wrote to his friends who were suffering, "I want to tell you something. You have a *living* hope, a hope based upon what Jesus Christ did when He arose from the grave. You see, He defeated the greatest enemy that man faces. He, by Himself, gained victory over death—and He promises that those who put their faith in Him shall also overcome death."

Are you looking for hope in difficult times? Are you trying to sort out the circumstances of your life? If so, look to Christ, because that is where hope is to be found.

Hope in the Midst of Hurt

But what do you say to a man who has laid to rest his wife of many years? The pain and hurt we feel as human beings can be almost indescribable . . . and yet a man who is a Christian has the hope that his believing wife is with the Lord.

What do you say to a woman who finds out she has a terminal disease and that, apart from some supernatural intervention, her days are numbered? If all we have to say to one another in our hopelessness and disillusionment are temporal and earthly platitudes, we are left with nothing. As Paul wrote to the Corinthians, "If in this life only we have hope in Christ, we are of all men the most pitiable" (1 Corinthians 15:19).

The only kind of hope the world has to offer is hope that ends at the grave. Yet the problems that cause us the greatest despair and hopelessness are those that begin, not end, at the grave. The mourning husband continues to hurt after the funeral. The daughter who loses her mother feels acute pain long after the graveside service. Where do we find hope for the kinds of problems that seem so prevalent in our lives?

Peter says it's found in a Person, the person of the Lord Jesus Christ. We pin our hope on Him because He is the only One who ever did what He did. He came out of death alive, victorious over the grave, and He promises us that if we put our trust in Him, even as He lives, we, too, shall live. There is hope in the midst of all the hurt!

No matter how dark our situation might become, our hope is anchored in Jesus Christ and in His power over death. Paul told us that if this is not true, our faith is useless, we're still in our sin, and we are without hope.

The reality of this came home to me recently when I read an article written by Joni Eareckson Tada. Joni is no stranger to tragedy and difficulty. Paralyzed in a diving accident at age seventeen, she has since ministered to millions across the world with the message of hope in Christ.

In an article she told about saying to her assistant one day, "File this, Francie, and make copies of this letter, would you? And, oh, yes, would you please pull out the sofa bed one more time?" Her paralysis blocks her body from feeling pain, and the only way she knows something is wrong is when her temperature and blood pressure begin to rise. She intuitively senses something is wrong. Oftentimes it's because she has unknowingly punctured her body or has rubbed against something and suffered a bruise or laceration. Sometimes she has to ask her assistant to undress her and examine her body to see what's wrong.

In the article Joni said she was in the midst of one of these episodes—they happen three or four times a month—and looked up to the ceiling and said aloud, "I want to quit this. Where do I go to resign from this stupid paralysis?"

As Francie was leaving the office that day she ducked out the door, then stuck her head back in and said, "I bet you can't wait for the Resurrection."

Joni wrote, "My eyes dampened again, but this time they were tears of relief and hope. I squeezed back my tears and dreamed what I've dreamed of a thousand times—the promise of the Resurrection. A flood of other hopeful promises filled my mind. *When we see him we shall be like him. . . . The perishable shall put on the imperishable. . . . The corruptible, that which is incorruptible . . . That which is sown in weakness will be raised in power. . . . He has given us an inheritance that can never perish, spoil, or fade.* I opened my eyes and said out loud with a smile, 'Come quickly, Lord Jesus.'"[3]

This hope of ours isn't merely "pie in the sky in the great by and by." It isn't merely a childish wish that we paint out in the far-flung future. It isn't merely that if we believe hard enough, things will get better. This is not "hope-so" hope; this is *know-so* hope. This is knowing the Person Who has done what no one else has ever done.

By virtue of that accomplishment, Jesus has laid claim to our faith and says, "If I came out of the grave victorious over death, and you put your trust in Me, you can have that same victory—not only over death, but in your life, day by day."

A Sure Hope

How sure is our hope? Notice what 1 Peter 1:4 says. This hope is "incorruptible and undefiled and . . . does not fade away, reserved in heaven for you." You know what? Those four traits are out of reach for anyone who places his or her hope in earthly things.

Have you ever noticed how disappointing placing your faith in human things can be? I confess that through the course of my life I have caught myself wrapping my hopes in various professional athletic teams.

When I attended Dallas Seminary, I got caught up in the Dallas Cowboys. I attended their Tuesday luncheons. I read every sports page about what was happening with the team. I knew everything about every player. I lived and died with the team.

Once they were in a crucial play-off game and, for some reason, the stadium hadn't sold out. When that happens, the game is not telecast in the city. Believe it or not, my long-suffering wife and I drove to Oklahoma and checked into a motel so we could watch the game from there. That's how committed I was!

But it got worse. In the early days of our family, I took my turn at cradling our small children. Donna finally made me quit holding them during football games because a couple of times I almost used them to throw a touchdown pass. I was really that wrapped up in the Cowboys! I followed them all the way to the summit . . . and then they lost! I was deeply depressed. Finally, of course, they won it all.

But you know what? Their victory left me surprisingly empty. I was glad they won, but . . .what now?

It's so easy to get wrapped up in things that can never truly reward our fondest hopes. Of course, I'm not for a moment suggesting that we shouldn't put our hope and trust in one another, that we should not bond strongly with our families. But there is a hope beyond that—and more important than that! That is the hope we place in the eternal God through His Son, Jesus Christ.

Peter says such a hope won't die. It won't decay, deteriorate, or be destroyed. That hope is there for you in the person of Jesus Christ; and because He is eternal, your hope in Him is eternal.

That's why there is such a distinctness to the way faithful Christian people respond to life. That's why they can handle the challenges that come their way. They may reel from the pressure, but down deep inside lies the quiet confidence that this, too, shall pass—and if it doesn't, it just gets better!

But What About Now?

You say, "Pastor Jeremiah, that's all well and good, and I'm glad about the future. That's going to be wonderful someday when we see the Lord and our hope is realized in an intimate, personal fellowship with Him. But I have to face next week. I get up in the morning and commute to a job that's terrorizing me. I have to live in a home situation that has me frantic. I have to deal with a disease that we can't control. How is my relationship with Jesus Christ going to make any difference in my life *now*? How does my hope about the future and eternity with Him affect the way I live *today*?"

Peter must have been anticipating that question, because he gave the answer in chapter 1, verse 5 of his first epistle. He says that we who have placed our hope in Christ are "kept by the power of God through faith for salvation ready to be revealed in the last time."

Now watch carefully. Here is how all the themes in this chapter work together. First of all, Peter says God has given us a hope that is secure, steadfast, and that can never be touched. It is beyond decay or destruction. Nothing can happen to it.

Second, in the very next verse Peter says God is committed to helping us fully realize that hope. God promises us a secure hope for our personal and eternal walk with Him and a day-by-day guarantee that He will keep us through the process of experiencing that hope. In fact, the word translated "kept" is one of the strongest terms in the New Testament. It literally means "to be garrisoned about by an army."

In other words, Peter says, "Here you are with your hope in Christ. You have fixed your eyes upon Him. You believe He came out of the grave, you trusted Him, and you believe that someday you, too, will live for eternity. But all the way along as you walk with Him, He has promised to keep you and to help you every day."

It's no wonder that many have written about the relationship between our eternal hope and our day-by-day experience of problems and difficulties. C. S. Lewis once said it this way: "Aim at Heaven and you will get earth 'thrown in': aim at earth and you will get neither."[4] That is a powerful truth. He means that if you don't choose the one and only path to heaven, you won't get there at all; and by missing heaven, you won't have anything worth living for down here either.

It's only as we fix our anchor in eternity that we find stability for life in these stress-filled days before our Lord's return. Oh, we'll still have problems. We're still in for a bumpy ride along the way. But there is a difference; our problems will finally begin to make sense.

A Reason for Trouble

Notice what Peter says in verses 6–7: "In this you greatly rejoice, though now for a little while, if need be, you have been grieved by various trials, that the genuineness of your faith, being much more precious than gold that perishes, though it is tested by fire, may be found to praise, honor, and glory at the revelation of Jesus Christ."

I like the Bible because it is so honest.

Peter isn't giving us some PMA stuff (Positive Mental Attitude) here. He isn't saying, "Get your hope up and everything is going to be all right." He's not saying, "If you put your trust in Christ, your problems will all go away." No. Instead he says, "Put your hope in the Lord and *get ready for some challenges*. Trials will come to rock you— but even in that process, God has a purpose."

A Scottish theologian named Samuel Rutherford once explained the purpose of the problems we face in the midst of our hope. His language may be Old English, but the truth he declared is critically important:

> If God had told me some time ago that he was about to make me as happy as I could be in this world, and then had told me he would begin by crippling me, in arm or limb or removing me from all my usual sources of enjoyment, I should have thought it a very strange mode of accomplishing his purpose. And yet, how is his wisdom manifest even in this? For if you should see a man shut up in a dark room, idolizing a set of lamps and rejoicing in their light, and you wish to make him truly happy, you would begin by blowing out all of his lamps and then throw open the shutters to let in the light of heaven.[5]

Joni Eareckson Tada read those words and added her own postscript:

> That's exactly what God did for me. When He sent a broken neck my way, He blew out the lamps in my life that lit up my here and now so captivatingly. The dark despair of my paralysis wasn't much fun, but it sure made those resurrection promises come alive! And one day when Jesus comes back, probably when I am in the middle of lying on my office sofa for the umpteenth time, God will throw open heaven's

shutters. I have no doubt I will be more ready for it then than I would have been if I had been on my feet.[6]

The problems we face and the difficult challenges of life only make us appreciate even more what it's going to be like when we see the Lord. As the lamps are put out, the glory of our wonderful Savior becomes even more precious to us.

We believers don't get by without the hurts, but there is a vast difference between how we and how nonbelievers process those difficulties. We are not shielded from great heaviness. Having hope in Christ doesn't mean we sail through life without storms. Hope in Christ won't keep us from feeling the tension and agonizing over the moral decay in these end times. Hope in Christ doesn't exempt us from the bumps and potholes of everyday living. If somebody tells you it does, he isn't living in the real world. Nobody gets through life without storms or bumps. We all experience heaviness. But here's the difference: *A Christian has superficial sorrow and central gladness; a nonbeliever has superficial gladness and central sorrow.*

A nonbeliever will do anything to stoke the fires of his superficial gladness. That is why he runs from one thing to the other, trying to keep the exterior alive for a moment to take away some of the pain within. Someone has said that a busy life is the anesthesia we use to deaden the pain of an empty life. But when the nonbeliever is alone, realizing where he is, he is overcome by a central sadness . . . a gnawing feeling of futility.

God wants to reverse all of that for you. He wants to take what's central to your life that is sad and replace it with joy. And He will do it through His Son, the Lord Jesus Christ.

It's a Decision

Sooner or later in all of our lives we come to a fork in the road where we have to make a choice. Either we go on putting our trust in our own strength and in that which others may offer us in the human realm, or we choose the other realm and make our journey toward God. Hope in God is a decision we make. It is something that we choose.

Norman Cousins was diagnosed with a very serious disease that threatened his life. All of his doctors told him he would die. He responded in a curious way to their announcement. He decided that if he was going to die, he would die *laughing*.

Cousins gathered the funniest cartoons he could find, all the Laurel and Hardy movies he could collect, all the joke books he could obtain, and spent eight to ten hours a day watching funny movies and laughing his head off. Guess what? He got better!

Afterward he wrote a book called *The Anatomy of an Illness* (W. W. Norton, 1995) in which he described the positive input of hope and laughter to physical illness. Subsequently Cousins was asked to join the medical faculty at the University of Southern California. For a decade he studied with these topflight medical practitioners, researching the idea of hope as a means of healing. He studied people with serious diagnoses, some with hope, others without it. He wrote a thick book based on his research called *Head First: The Biology of Hope*. What Cousins discovered is astonishing.

In one passage he writes,

> People tell me not to offer hope unless I know hope to be real, but I don't have the power not to respond to an outstretched hand. I don't know enough to say that hope can't be real. I'm not sure anyone knows enough to deny hope. I have seen too many cases these past ten years when death predictions were delivered from high professional station only to be gloriously refuted by patients having less to do with tangible biology than with the human spirit.[7]

Cousins said that while "the human spirit" may be a vague idea to some, it is probably the greatest force in the human arsenal for dealing with discouragement and disease. That is why, when confronted with people who were told their situations were terminal, he would reply, "Don't deny the diagnosis, but defy the verdict."[8]

I wonder, How many of us have faced challenges like that? Everybody around us is declaring how bad it's going to be and why it won't work and how we can't do it. Everyone talks about how our culture is in moral free fall and we might as well stock up on dehydrated food and live in a root cellar in North Dakota.

My friend, we cannot deny the diagnosis, but through faith in Jesus Christ, we *can* defy the verdict. Last I knew, the final word on hope didn't come from the earth, but from *heaven*.

Still, we have to choose hope. Too often, we choose lies instead.

Martin Seligman wrote a book titled *Learned Optimism*. Seligman says that we *learn* to be hopeless. When difficulty strikes, we tell ourselves three lies about what's going on: It's *personal*, it's *pervasive*, and it's *permanent*.[9]

When we are in despair, too often we tell ourselves the disaster is personal. "I'm the only person in the world who has ever gone through this," we say. "It must be some kind of personal vendetta God has against me. *Lord, why me?*"

Then we tell ourselves it's pervasive, that this one difficult thing in our lives has affected everything else. Our whole lives are messed up because of the one thing that's wrong. Have you ever felt like that? You're going through some tough times and you find yourself saying, "My whole life is just one big mess." That's probably not true. There may be one corner of your life that's pretty messy right now, but your whole life probably is not a mess.

But the worst lie we tell ourselves is the last one, that it's permanent. "It's awful. It's bad—and it's not ever going to get better." And by the time we have taken ownership of those lies, we're both hopeless and helpless.

Why do we do this to ourselves? Why not choose hope instead?

A Door of Hope

The prophet Hosea talked about a time in the future when God will wonderfully bless the Jews, the people of Israel. Notice what he says in Hosea 2:15: "I will give . . . the Valley of Achor as a door of hope; she shall sing there."

This is an astonishing promise. Why? Because the Valley of Achor is the place where Israel first met defeat after entering the promised land. Remember the story? An Israelite named Achan disobeyed God and brought judgment on Israel. When his sin was finally uncovered, he and his whole family were stoned in the Valley of Achor.

In Hebrew, *Achor* means "trouble." Joshua 7:26 concludes the sad story by noting, "Therefore that place has been called the Valley of Achor ever since" (NIV).

But centuries later Hosea predicts things are going to be so great for the people of Israel that the very valley where Achan was stoned—the Valley of Trouble—will become "a door of hope."

Do you know what I've discovered? Every time a Christian goes through the Valley of Trouble, there is always a door of hope.

Now, if you want to wallow in the Valley of Trouble for the rest of your life, feeling a sense of hopelessness and a loss of blessing, you can do that. But do this first: Look around in the Valley of Trouble. *There is a door.* It's a door of hope. If you want to leave the Valley of Trouble, you must go through the door of hope. You must decide to take action. When you do, you'll walk out of the Valley of Trouble through the door of hope and back into the wide place of God's blessing.

Satan will tell you, "No, you're in the valley and you've got to stay there. You can't get out. It's a valley with no exit."

I don't know how many Christian people I've met through the life of my ministry who have been in the valley for ten or fifteen years.

When you finally figure out what got them in there and how easy it would be for them to walk through the door of hope into God's blessing, you wonder, *Why didn't somebody tell them?*

No, my friend. Hope grows out of hopelessness. You may feel stuck in the Valley of Trouble, but there is always a door! You must simply decide to go through it.

Jesus is coming! He will come back for His own, and we will see Him face-to-face. And until that time, the Son of God lives within us and has promised to walk with us and never forsake us.

He lives! Hope is alive!

Because He Lives

One of my favorite people is Bill Gaither. He and his wife, Gloria, have given us much of the modern hymnody that we enjoy. It's a great heritage.

Bill tells how back in the early sixties, he and Gloria were going through some terribly difficult days. He had just endured a bout with mononucleosis; Gloria was suffering with mild depression; they were about to have a child. Gloria looked around at a world that seemed in utter turmoil and her heart filled with despair. Here this child was coming into their home and she thought, *What kind of people are we to bring a child into this messed-up world?*

One day she was in her study, quiet and waiting before the Lord, and the Spirit of God began to move upon her heart. He impressed upon her this central message of hope in Jesus Christ. He began to help her understand that life always conquers death—as long as that life is in Christ. Soon she began to grasp that life would conquer death, not just someday, but *now*. She saw that if we place our faith in the living Christ, we can conquer feelings of discouragement and depression prompted by the challenges of everyday life. She was so overcome by this realization that she tried to express it in the lyrics of a song, a hymn that has become very precious to us all. It goes like this:

Because He lives I can face tomorrow.
Because He lives all fear is gone.
Because I know He holds the future
and life is worth the living just because He lives.

And now you also know why she wrote the second verse of that song:

How sweet to hold our newborn baby,
and feel the pride and joy he gives.
But greater still the calm assurance
our child can face uncertain days because He lives.

One day after the song was written, Bill's father visited the Gaithers in Alexandria. He came into the office building where Gloria was working and said, "Hey, get Bill and come out here. I've got something to show you."

Just a few weeks before his visit, the parking lot at the building had been resurfaced. Workers had brought in stone, laid it down, and rolled it out with heavy machinery. Then they came in with pea gravel, also rolling it out. Next they covered the stone and gravel with hot, molten asphalt, rolled it, then finished by putting down and rolling another layer of asphalt.

Bill's father pointed to the middle of the parking lot and said, "Look at that!" Sure enough, right up through the rock, right up through the pea gravel, right up through the first layer of asphalt and right up through the second, had grown a tender, green shoot. It wasn't huge or substantial. A child could have reached down and plucked it out. But the shoot didn't come up because it was strong or sharp or because it had any special ability. It came up through that stone and gravel and asphalt because it had one quality: *life*. Life always reigns over no life![10]

Jesus Christ speaks to all of us today as we seek the hope we need for stable, positive, productive lives. Even in these tumultuous times, He reaches out to us and says, "Listen! I am the living God. I overcame death. I want to live within you and give you the hope you need to face the challenges of life."

If you have never put your hope in God through faith in His Son, Jesus Christ, you need to make that decision. That is where life begins! You can run to all kinds of psychological remedies for the hopelessness in your life, but if you do not know the risen Christ, you cannot find or enjoy ultimate hope . . . and you will continue to live at the corner of Hopelessness and Despair.

Whatever your circumstances today, whatever the weather, whatever situations press in on you, step out into the bright, warm sunlight of a hope that is alive. It is alive because He is alive, and it will never die because He lives forever.

And never forget my friend, before this day is over, before the sun sets over the hills, before you scratch another day off your calendar, He may call us all to Himself. In the twinkling of an eye, you will find yourself wrapped in the strong arms of Hope Himself.

Maybe today!

Epilogue

─────── ❧ ───────

OF WHOM SHALL I BE AFRAID?

And in the midst of the seven lampstands [stood] One like the Son of Man, clothed with a garment down to the feet and girded about the chest with a golden band. His head and His hair were white like wool, as white as snow, and His eyes like a flame of fire; His feet were like fine brass, as if refined in a furnace, and His voice as the sound of many waters; He had in His right hand seven stars, out of His mouth went a sharp two-edged sword, and His countenance was like the sun shining in its strength. And when I saw Him, I fell at His feet as dead. But He laid His right hand on me, saying to me, "Do not be afraid; I am the First and the Last. I am He who lives, and was dead, and behold, I am alive forevermore. Amen. And I have the keys of Hades and of Death." (Revelation 1:13–18)

Revelation chapter 1 contains an awesome portrait of the risen and glorified Christ. Jesus Christ, the Alpha and the Omega, the First and the Last, appeared to the apostle John in a heart-stopping vision—not as the meek and tender Lamb of God, but as the roaring Lion of Judah. Verses 13 through 16 paint a picture of an almighty Savior shining in the fullness of His power and glory:

His clothes spoke of His greatness, faithfulness, and majesty;

His head and hair of gleaming white spoke of His eternity and holiness;

His eyes of fire spoke of His omniscience;

His feet of brass spoke of His powerful justice;

His mouth spoke of His supreme sovereignty over the world;

His hands spoke of His lordship, control, and authority;

His face, the central feature of His person, made everything fade in the light of its brilliance.

Commentator William Ramsey captured the awesome scene like this:

Here is the Son of Man clothed with power and majesty, with awe and terror. That long royal robe; that golden belt buckled at the breast; that hair so glistening white that like snow on which the sun is shining, it hurts the eye; those eyes flashing of fire, eyes which read every heart and penetrate every hidden corner; those feet glowing in order to trample down the wicked; that loud reverberating voice, like the mighty breakers booming against the rocky shore of Patmos; that sharp, long and heavy great-sword with two biting edges; yes, that entire appearance "as the sun shines in its power," too intense for human eyes to stare at—the entire picture, taken as a whole, is symbolic of Christ, the Holy One, coming to purge His churches.[1]

John tells us he was so overcome by this majestic vision that "when I saw him, I fell at his feet as dead." This was no voluntary act of worship, but an instinctive reaction of fear. Others in the Bible experienced the same fear: Abraham "fell on his face" when God spoke with him (Genesis 17:3); Moses "hid his face, for he was afraid" (Exodus 3:6); Balaam "bowed his head and fell flat on his face"

(Numbers 22:31); Joshua "fell on his face to the earth and worshiped" (Joshua 5:14); Gideon and Manoah cried out in alarm lest they should die (Judges 6:22–23; 13:20–22); Isaiah felt that he was undone (Isaiah 6:5); Ezekiel fell on his face (Ezekiel 1:28); Daniel felt like a man who had been drained of all his strength (Daniel 10:8).

And the situation did not change in the days of the New Testament. The three disciples at the Transfiguration saw Jesus' face shine as the sun and "fell on their faces and were greatly afraid" (Matthew 17:6); Saul of Tarsus fell to the ground and was left blind as a result of witnessing His glory (Acts 22:7,11).

So even though John had known this Jesus personally and had laid his head upon His breast, it is no surprise that he fell at Jesus' feet as dead. He was overwhelmed by the majesty of the glorified Son of man.

Ah, but Jesus would not allow His servant and friend to stay in that position! John tells us the Master "laid His right hand on me, saying to me, 'Do not be afraid. . . .'" In the midst of John's paralyzing fear, the Lord touched him with His right hand, which held the stars, and spoke to him with the voice that roared like the sound of many waters. Both the touch and the words greatly encouraged the apostle.

This would have been enough, but the Lord in His grace then gave John three mighty reasons why he should not be afraid:

1. Do not be afraid, for I am the eternal God. "I am the First and the Last," Jesus proclaimed. "I am He who lives." In other words, "I am First in that no one is before Me. And I am Last in that none will follow Me. I am the living One! So do not be afraid, for I live forever!"

2. Do not be afraid, for I am the resurrected Christ. "I . . . was dead, and behold, I am alive forevermore," the Lord announced. This is the central fact that gave the apostle Peter hope; this is why he could tell us we have been born into a living hope. Jesus has risen from the dead! And therefore death has no more power over us. "Do not be afraid," Jesus tells us, "for I have overcome death!"

3. Do not be afraid, for I own the keys of death and hell. "I have the keys of Hades and of Death," Jesus declared. To possess these keys means that our Lord triumphed over death and the grave. "So do not be afraid," Jesus tells us, "for the power over death and the grave is in My hand, and is available to all who trust in Me!"

Friend, this is the Jesus whose sure prophetic words we have been studying together. This is the Jesus who not only knows the future, but who lives in it just as comfortably as He lives in what has been. This is the Jesus who holds all power in His hands, and yet who bids us draw near and walk with Him. And this is the Jesus who sees everything that lies ahead for every one of us and who says to us all, "Do not be afraid!"

In the end, that is His final word for each of us. Oh, trials will come. Kingdoms will fall. The very heavens will be shaken. But because He is Who He is, He encourages us with the same words of power He gave to the apostle John: "Do not be afraid!" And so we may confidently say with the psalmist,

> The LORD is my light and my salvation; whom shall I fear? The LORD is the strength of my life; of whom shall I be afraid? (Psalm 27:1)

Notes

Chapter 1

1. William R. Macklin, "Judgement Day Fails to Arrive on Time," *The Sunday Oregonian,* 2 October 1994.

2. Nick Harrison, "Gearing Up for Millennial Fervor," *Publishers Weekly,* 13 January 1997, 38.

3. Ibid., 40.

4. Larry Burkett, "Awaiting the 'Churn' of the Century," *Turning Point,* August 1998, 13.

5. Richard Lacayo, "The End of the World As We Know It?" *Time,* 18 January 1999, 64.

6. Ibid. 68.

7. Burkett, "'Churn' of the Century."

Chapter 2

1. Herbert Schlossberg, *Idols for Destruction* (New York: Thomas Nelson, 1983), 234.

2. Ibid.

3. The story of deception in the time of Josiah and Ezekiel is adapted from *Invasion of Other Gods: The Seduction of New Age Spirituality,* by David Jeremiah with C. C. Carlson (Dallas: Word, 1995), 47.

4. David Crum, "Bible Isn't Jesus' Gospel Truth, Scholars Say," *Orange County Register,* 12 December 1993.

5. David Breese, *His Infernal Majesty* (Chicago: Moody Press, 1974), 19.

6. Ibid., 26.

7. Warren W. Wiersbe, *The Strategy of Satan: How to Detect and Defeat Him* (Wheaton, Ill.: Tyndale, 1979), 21–22.

8. Breese, *His Infernal Majesty,* 38–39.

Chapter 3

1. National Center for Victims of Crime, 2111 Wilson Blvd., Suite 300, Arlington, VA 22201, 1998.

2. J. R. Church, "Riders of Revelation 6, Mount Up!" in *Foreshocks of Antichrist*, William T. James ed. (Eugene, Ore.: Harvest House Publishers, 1997), 332–33.

3. Summarized from the Center for Disease Control Semiannual HIV/AIDS Surveillance Report. Numbers are based on AIDS cases reported to CDC through June 30, 1998.

Chapter 4

1. Timothy George, "The Lure of the Apocalypse," *Christianity Today*, 19 June 1995, 16.

2. Ibid.

3. William A. Alnor, *Soothsayers of the Second Advent* (Old Tappan, N.J.: Revell Co., 1989), 35–36.

4. Ibid., 36.

5. Lester Sumrall, *I Predict 2000 A.D.* (South Bend, Ind.: LeSEA Publishing Co., 1987), 74.

6. William David Spencer, "Does Anyone Really Know What Time It Is?" *Christianity Today*, 17 July 1995, 29.

7. Charles Swindoll, *Rise and Shine* (Portland, Ore.: Multnomah, 1989), 168–69.

8. Wendy Murray Zoba, "Future Tenses," *Christianity Today*, 2 October 1995, 22.

Chapter 5

1. A. W. Tozer, *Man: The Dwelling Place of God* (Camp Hill, Penn.: Christian Publications, 1966), 151.

2. "On the Mountain's Brink," U.S. Dept. of Agriculture booklet, 25.

3. Row Findley, "St. Helens: Mountain with a Death Wish," *National Geographic,* January 1981, 20.

Chapter 6

1. Laurence J. Peter and Raymond Hull, *The Peter Principle* (New York: Bantam, 1969), 7.

Chapter 7

1. Charles Panati, *Panati's Extraordinary Endings of Practically Everything and Everybody* (New York: Harper & Row, 1989), 398.

2. Ferris Daniel Whitesell, *Basic New Testament Evangelism* (Grand Rapids, Mich.: Zondervan, 1949), 133.

3. Adapted from John M. Drescher, "A Plea for Fishing," *Pulpit Digest,* July/August 1978.

Chapter 8

1. Patrick M. Morley, "Building Our Kids," in *God's Vitamin "C" for the Spirit of Men,* comp. D. Larry Miller (Lancaster, Penn.: Starburst Publishers, 1996), 81.

Chapter 9

1. Robin Jones, retold by Casandra Lindell, "A Parable of God's Perspective," *More Stories for the Heart,* comp. Alice Gray (Sisters, Ore.: Multnomah, 1997), 270-71.

Chapter 10

1. Douglas Cooligan, "That Helpless Feeling: The Dangers of Stress," *New York Magazine,* 14 July 1975, 28.

2. Mike Bellah, "Make Room for Baby Boomers," *The Evangelical Beacon,* April 1991, 7.

3. Joni Earckson Tada, "We Will Be Whole," *Today's Christian Woman,* March/April 1991, 35.

4. C. S. Lewis, *Mere Christianity* (New York: MacMillan, 1966), 118.

5. Tada, "We Will Be Whole," 36.

6. Ibid.

7. Norman Cousins, *Head First: The Biology of Hope* (New York: E. P. Dutton, 1989), 65.

8. Ibid., 239.

9. Martin E. P. Seligman, *Learned Optimism* (New York: Pocket Books, 1998), 40–51.

10. Gloria Gaither, *Because He Lives* (Grand Rapids, Mich.: Zondervan, 1997), 16, 21–22.

Epilogue

1. W. Hendriksen, *More than Conquerors: An Interpretation of the Book of Revelation* (Grand Rapids, Mich.: Baker Book House, 1940), 71.

Subject Index

2000. *See* year 2000

Abraham, 166–167
absolute truth, 36
Achan, 187
Achor, Valley of, 187–188
adultery, 36
afraid, do not be, 193–194
AIDS, 48
Anatomy of an Illness, 185
angels, 71–72
antichrist
    as deceiver, 41
    as lawless one, 58–59
    as man of sin, 41
    spirit of, 47

Armageddon, 80
Asherah, 28, 29

Baal, 28
baby boomers, 173
Barclay, William, 93
"Because He Lives", 188–189
Bellah, Mike, 173
bema seat. *See* judgment seat of Christ
biblical tension, 159
Breese, David, 33, 39
Burkett, Larry, 4, 11

calendar errors, 66
Camping, Harold, 3
Christian Century, 64

Scripture Index

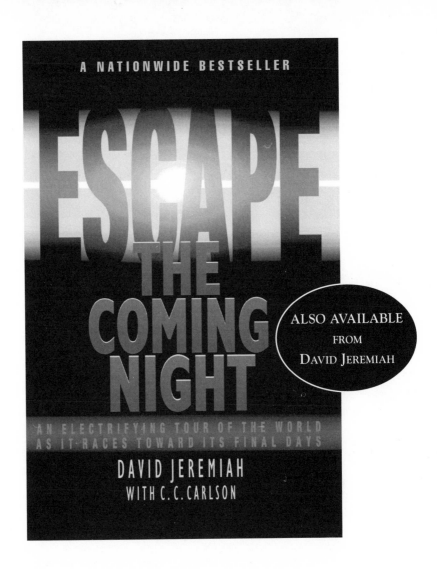

AN ELECTRIFYING TOUR OF THE WORLD AS IT
RACES TOWARD ITS FINAL DAYS

No one can deny that the world is in trouble, but how do we explain so
much chaos or live with such turmoil? Is there any hope for peace in
our time? In this dramatic narrative on the Book of Revelation, Dr.
David Jeremiah answers these and many more challenging questions,
guiding the reader on an electrifying tour of a world careening headlong into the twenty-first century.

WORD PUBLISHING
Available at Bookstores Everywhere.